CW01669163

THE COMPLET
GUIDE TO
PORTFOLIO

Other books by Barry Thomas:

A PostScript Cookbook, Macmillan, ISBN 0 333 48478 9

A Layout DDL Primer, TTP, ISBN 1 871915 00 7

THE COMPLETE BEGINNER'S GUIDE TO THE ATARI PORTFOLIO

Barry Thomas

Alan Thomas

First Published 1989

Published by THOMAS TECHNICAL PUBLICATIONS LTD, Copestake Cottage, Pinfold Lane, Bradley, ASHBOURNE, Derbyshire, DE6 1PN.

Printed in the UK by Commercial Colour Press, London.

British Library Cataloguing in Publication Data

Thomas, Barry, *1958-*
The complete beginner's guide to the Atari Portfolio
1. Atari microcomputer systems
I. Title II. Thomas. Alan, *1962-*
004.16

ISBN 1 871915 05 8

CONTENTS

PREFACE

Back in the days when computers were the size of a room and consumed enormous amounts of electricity, people probably sat around, bathed in the light (and heat) from row upon row of gently glowing valves, and mused how one day, computers would be so small they could be carried around in a suitcase.

Sure enough, that day came. The luggable computer had arrived. Still requiring mains electricity though, the luggable computer was transportable, but not exactly lightweight. Then came the battery operated computer. The real portable had arrived. People could be seen on trains and planes, running their favourite software and being thought awfully modern.

However, even the battery operated computer was quite heavy, and the batteries would give you a few hours operation, but little more. Still the **really** portable computer had not arrived. Until now.

There have been other pocket sized computers, but they were almost always based on proprietary hardware and software. Each manufacturer had its own design and operating system. You could use any of these computers in conjunction with a desk-top computer, but the two were quite different animals. Compatibility with the industry-standard IBM PC was not part of the equation when designing or selling pocket computers.

Now we have the Portfolio which is specifically designed to work closely with an IBM compatible desk-top pc. The files on the two computers are stored in exactly the same format and the Portfolio will run software designed to run on the pc.

The Portfolio's built in spreadsheet is file compatible with the industry-standard spreadsheet, Lotus 1-2-3. At last the pocket computer is beginning to look like a truly valuable part of the pc user's armoury. And then there is the Portfolio's built-in text editor, calculator, calendar, diary and address book. The pocket computer has come of age.

This book shows how to make your work easier and more productive by using the Portfolio. There are sections on each of the built-in applications, and lots of hints and tips on how to make them work best with your desk-top pc.

This book is for Andrew and Susan Ramsden.

1

GETTING STARTED

WHAT IS THE PORTFOLIO?

The Atari Portfolio is a fully fledged computer. Just a few years ago, a computer with less memory than the Portfolio, no application software, no built-in file storage and occupying half your desk would have cost ten times and weighed twenty times as much as the Portfolio does today.

The Portfolio has a powerful suite of built-in programs. These allow you to write and edit documents, carry out complex financial tasks, keep as many different address-book files as you like, maintain a diary complete with appointment alarms and generally take your computing with you wherever you go.

The Portfolio uses an operating and filing system compatible with the industry standard PC/MS-DOS, and has a Worksheet which creates files compatible with the industry standard Lotus 1-2-3.

If you are new to computers, the Portfolio is easy to use. If you are an old hand, the Portfolio is still easy to use but will also do many of the things you thought only a desk-top computer could do.

Enough of the chat. Let's go straight ahead and look at the Portfolio itself.

SETTING UP

Inserting the Batteries

The Atari Portfolio runs on three AA size batteries. The best type to use are the alkaline type which have the longest life. To fit the batteries, first make sure the Portfolio is closed. Place the Portfolio face down on a flat surface and pop out the battery compartment cover on the hinge side of the casing.

Insert three batteries as indicated inside the battery compartment. Replace the battery compartment cover.

Replacing the Batteries

When the power of the batteries becomes low (after 6 to 8 weeks regular use), the Portfolio warns you of the low power with a message on the screen. You should then replace the batteries with a new set as soon as possible. For this reason it is wise to always carry a spare set of batteries.

Getting Ready

The Portfolio is a robust computer. It's only moving part is the hinge between the two halves of the casing. However, when using any computer, it is wise to observe the following precautions:

- **Do** handle the Portfolio carefully
- **Do** keep the casing, keyboard and screen clean

- **Don't** use the Portfolio anywhere excessively dusty
- **Don't** get the Portfolio wet.

The last point may seem obvious, but one very easy way to get a computer wet is to spill a cup of coffee over it while you are working... you have been warned!

The First Screen

When you have inserted the batteries as described above, turn the Portfolio over and slide the catch on the front edge to open the casing.

Open the casing to a convenient working angle. The screen shows the following copyright message:

```
Copyright (c) 1989 DIP
Distributed Information Processing Ltd
Surrey Research Park, Guildford, England
All rights reserved
Tous droits réservés
Alle Rechte vorbehalten

BIOS: X.XXX    Operating System: X.XXX
```

After a few seconds, the screen changes to show:

```
Keyboard - Clavier - Tastatur

Type "E" for English    (QWERTY)
Type "F" pour Français  (AZERTY)
Type "D" für Deutsch    (QWERTZ)
```

By pressing E, F or D you select the keyboard layout and language which the Portfolio then uses. This isn't a 'once and for all' decision, the language can be changed at any time. This will be explained later on in chapter 9.

Select the language you want to use by pressing E for English, F for Français and D for Deutsch. The screen then shows in the appropriate language a prompt for the current date:

```
Date: Tue 1-01-1980
New Date (mm-dd-yy)
```

Type in today's date in the format shown on the screen, then press the [Return] key (the L shaped key at the right of the keyboard). The screen then prompts for the time:

```
Time: 0:00:00.00
```

Type in the correct time in the format hh:mm:ss. The last pair of digits are for the hundredths of a second. Again press the [Return] key. For example, if the time is 3.45 pm, type:

```
15:45 [Return]
```

The screen then shows:

```
DIP Operating System X.XX vX.XXX
Copyright (c) DIP 1989

c>
```

The last item on the screen is the DOS prompt. DOS is the Portfolio's operating and filing system and is fully explained in chapter 4.

THE KEYBOARD

The Portfolio's keyboard follows the usual typewriter layout, with the numeric keys across the top. The [Return] key mentioned earlier is the L shaped key at the right of the keyboard. There are a number of other special keys which allow you to use various features of the Portfolio, but one worth of mention now is the [/I\] key at the lower left corner.

The [/I\] key gives you access to the features of the Portfolio which do not appear on an ordinary desk-top pc. One of these is the screen contrast control, described below. Also

the *cursor* keys, the four keys marked with arrows at the lower right corner of the keyboard.

THE SCREEN

The Portfolio's screen is a super-twist LCD displaying 8 lines, each with 40 columns. To make the screen easy to read, the Portfolio has a contrast control. To increase or decrease the screen contrast, hold down the [/I\] key and press the [↑] or [↓] key at the lower right corner of the keyboard. You may need to press these keys a number of times to set the screen contrast to just the desired level.

The 40x8 format of the screen can also be used as a 'window' onto a larger screen, 25 lines by 80 columns. This feature is fully described in chapter 9.

THE MEMORY CARD DRIVE

Most desk-top pc's use disks to store information. The Portfolio uses solid-state memory cards. These are the size of a credit card and are used in the same way as a disk. You can store any information from the Portfolio on a memory card. The cards can be erased, rewritten, and used over and over.

Memory cards have a battery which keeps your information safe for up to one year. The cards are available in a range of capacities and come with full instructions.

The slot at the left hand side of the Portfolio's keyboard is the Portfolio's memory card drive.

THE EXPANSION PORT

At the right of the Portfolio's keyboard is a clip-on cover which reveals an expansion port. Various optional devices can be plugged in here, including a connector which allows your Portfolio to transfer information to and from a desk-top pc.

2

THE APPLICATIONS

WHAT IS AN APPLICATION?

The Portfolio has a number of built-in programs which supply facilities usually found only on expensive desk-top computers. These are called the *application* programs. This chapter briefly describes how to start the programs, how they operate and their common features.

Each of the applications is described in some detail in the following chapters, but you are recommended to read this chapter first for an overview of what the applications do and how they work.

The applications are all available from a menu. You can select one application, then return to the menu and select another. However, you can also start any of the applications from the DOS prompt or from within any other activity.

HOW INFORMATION IS STORED

Before we look at the applications themselves, we should first know a little about how information is stored in the Portfolio by the application programs.

There are four application programs which store information in the Portfolio's memory. These are the Address Book, the Diary, the Editor and the Worksheet. They store information in the Portfolio's memory in the form of *files*.

What is a File?

A computer file is rather like a card file you slip into a filing cabinet. It is a self-contained unit and contains information on a particular subject. It might be the minutes from a meeting or a list of all the company's employees.

If you want to start a new file for new subject, just like taking a new clean card folder, the Portfolio allows you to do so. Similarly, if the information in a file becomes out of date or no longer wanted, the whole file can simply and quickly be deleted.

However, once a file has been deleted, it has then gone for good! A file should only be deleted when you are sure you no longer need its contents.

File Names

Each file stored in the Portfolio is given a *file name*. A file name may be up to eight characters long. File names can consist of letters or numbers or a mixture, for example:

```
LETTER1        EMPLOYMT
JOB-25-3       BANKLETR
```

Notice that the files are given names which are relevant to their contents. If you name your files **0001**, **0002**, **0003** and so on, you might get a little confused when looking for the file containing a letter to your bank manager. So choose names which reflect the contents of the files in question - it makes life much easier later on. Also, if you write a lot of letters to the bank, it makes sense to give them similar names, perhaps **bnkaug01** (bank: August 1), **bnkaug02** (bank: August 2), **bnksep01** (bank: September 1) and so on. This means that you can refer to groups of files whose names start with the same letters. More on this topic later.

As an extra guide to the contents of a particular file, you can also add a *file extension*. A file extension may consist of up to three letters and numbers and is separated from the file name by a dot (.). The application programs automatically add their own file extensions as follows:

Address Book files	**.adr**
Diary files	**.dry**
Editor files	**.txt**
Worksheet files	**.wks**

You can create files in a variety of ways which have different file extensions to these, but the applications always use these extensions unless you specify otherwise.

Directories

When you are storing your card files in a filing cabinet, you might also organise them in larger groups in the separate drawers of the cabinet. For example, the top drawer might be used for all of your letters, the middle drawer for the accounts and the bottom drawer for your employment and personnel records.

In just the same way, you can organise the files in the Portfolio's memory into *directories*. A directory is just like a drawer in a filing cabinet: it can hold a large number of files, it organises your storage space and makes finding a particular file much easier.

Each directory has a *directory name* which may consist of up to eight letters and numbers, and can have an extension like an ordinary file.

The advantage of the Portfolio over a filing cabinet is that you can have as many directories (drawers) as you like, you can add another directory at any time, you can remove directories and you can have directories within directories!

The Portfolio's internal memory, where the directories are created, is in fact a directory itself, but this one is special. This directory, referred to as the *root level directory*, does not have a normal directory name and it cannot be removed. The Portfolio allows you to have as many directories as you like in the root level directory and also a large number of ordinary files - just like any other directory.

Let's take the example of a single file; a letter to the bank. The text of the letter is in a file called **bnkaug01.txt**. The file is in a directory called **banklet** which is stored at the root level directory.

To create a new directory on a drive, you must use the DOS command **md** (make directory). This and the other DOS commands are described in detail in chapter 4.

The Portfolio's Drives

To complete our knowledge of how the Portfolio organises files, we must know about *drives*. The name comes from when all computers had disk drives - into which were placed floppy disks. Each disk drive was given a letter, a, b, c and so on.

Now the word drive refers to either a *memory card drive*, into which is put a *memory card* which acts like a disk, or an area of the Portfolio's memory which acts like a disk drive as described earlier. Directories and files are created on these drives, which can be written to and read just like a disk drive on a desk-top computer. The internal drive, also called a *RAM drive* (because it is made up of RAM; Random Access Memory), is referred to as **c:**. The drive letter followed by a colon is called the *drive designator.*

This drive designator is used to preface the file and directory names used above, but again, more of this in chapter 4.

The Portfolio's Memory

So far we have talked about the Portfolio's memory as if it were all available for the storage of files. In fact the memory has two main functions, for storing your files and for running programs. If you want to know more about the details of managing the Portfolio's memory, including the use of directories, refer to chapter 4.

STARTING THE APPLICATIONS

There are a number of ways in which to start any of the applications. The method you use depends upon what the Portfolio is being used for at the time.

Starting an Application from DOS

When the DOS prompt (`c>`)is shown on the screen you can display the main applications menu by typing:

```
app [Return]
```

or by holding down the [/|\] key and pressing [Z].

Note that where [Return] appears in this book, it means a single press of the [Return] key, the L shaped key at the right of the keyboard.

The screen shows:

```
(c) DIP 1989 49437
Address Book
Calculator
Diary
Editor
Setup
Worksheet
```

This is the main applications menu. You can select any of the applications by just pressing the first letter of the application name. So to enter the Calculator, press [C], or to enter the Diary, press [D]. A later section in this chapter goes into detail on the menus and windows used by the Portfolio.

To return to the applications menu from any of the applications, press [Esc] (Escape).

When the DOS prompt is on the screen, you can use the **app** command as described above to go straight into one of the applications without going via the applications menu. Type the **app** command as before but followed by a space, a slash (/) and the initial letter of the application:

Type	**Application selected**
`app /a [Return]`	Address book
`app /c [Return]`	Calculator
`app /d [Return]`	Diary
`app /e [Return]`	Editor
`app /s [Return]`	Setup
`app /w [Return]`	Worksheet

Strictly speaking, Setup is not an application program, but a facility for making a number of software and hardware settings so that the Portfolio works in just the way you want.

The **app** command, with or without a following slash and initial, can be used in exactly the same way from within a *batch file*. See chapter 4 for details of batch files.

Starting an Application with the [/|\] key

Any of the applications can be started at any time - whatever the current operation, by holding down the [/|\] key and pressing:

Press	**For the**
[A]	Address Book
[C]	Calculator
[D]	Diary
[E]	Editor
[S]	Setup
[W]	Worksheet
[Z]	Applications Menu

This means that you can be using the Address Book to look up a telephone number, then jump straight into the Worksheet by pressing [/|\] [W]; you might be checking some figures in the Worksheet and need to type a quick note in the Editor - just press [/|\] [E].

When you then exit from the most recently used application, you return either to DOS or to the applications menu, whichever was used at the start of this chain of operations.

The only exception to this is that you cannot jump **from** Setup, however, you can jump **into** Setup from any of the applications.

Note that if you are in an application where the information in the current file has been changed, perhaps you added an Address Book entry or deleted some text from a document in the Editor, when you try to jump to another application, you will first be offered the chance to save the document as usual.

THE SCREEN LAYOUT

The built-in applications have a common screen layout. The screen is bounded by a frame. This frame contains certain information about the file in use; the current date and time and the state of the keyboard (whether CAP lock or NUM lock is in use and so on).

This screen is from the Worksheet, but the following description applies to all applications:

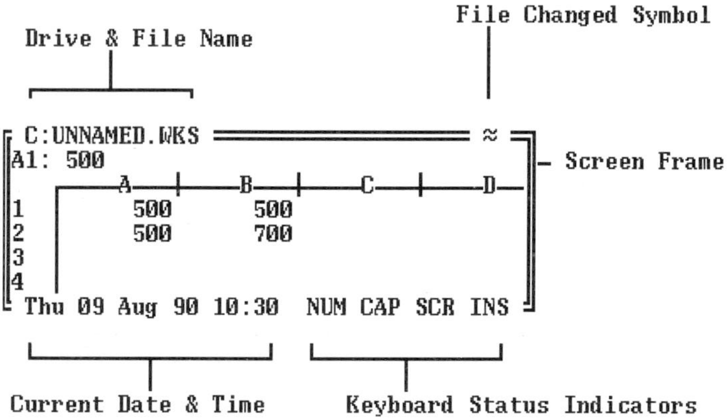

The Screen Frame

The screen frame is a double line all round the edge of the screen. The frame contains the date and time and some other information. The frame can be removed at any time in any application by holding down the [Fn] key and pressing [5] (Function key 5). Press the same key again to return the frame and its information.

The Current Date & Time

The current date and time are taken from the Portfolio's internal clock calendar. The time displayed in the frame is updated every minute.

To change the date or time, see the **date** and **time** commands in chapter 4.

The Drive & File Name

The current drive and the name of the current file are shown on the top line of the screen at the left hand side. In the example above, the current drive is **c:**, the file name is **unnamed** and the extension is **.wks**. The last two are separated by a dot.

The Portfolio automatically gives a new, blank file the name **unnamed**. You can give it a more meaningful name yourself according to its contents. For example, **letter1**, **jobcosts** and so on.

As we saw earlier in this chapter, the four applications which use files, the Address Book, Diary, Editor and Worksheet, have their own file extensions:

Application	Extension
Address Book	**.adr**
Diary	**.dry**
Editor	**.txt**
Worksheet	**.wks**

So a file called **jobcost.wks** is a Worksheet file, and one called **letter1.txt** is a text file from the Editor.

The File Changed Symbol

At the top right of the screen, the 'file changed' symbol may appear. This means that some information in the current file has been changed since the last time the file was saved. The symbol appears as soon as you start adding information to or deleting information from a new file, or changing an existing file.

When you save the current file, the symbol is removed, leaving just the usual frame in its place.

The Keyboard Status Indicators

The keyboard can be set into various modes. An indicator appears at the bottom right of the screen frame when any of these modes is selected: CAP (Caps Lock), NUM (Num Lock), INS (Insert mode), SCR (Scroll Lock).

MENUS & WINDOWS

All of the built-in programs use a system of menus to carry out commands. For example, press [/I\] [Z] to view the applications menu. This is the first menu you see on the Portfolio, and it looks like this:

```
(c) DIP 1989 49437
Address Book
Calculator
Diary
Editor
Setup
Worksheet
```

The first time the applications menu is selected, the top line shows the software version number, thereafter it shows the amount of free memory in the Portfolio.

The menu is displayed in a *window*. The current operation, whether it is an application, a menu or an error message, is always shown in a double-lined window.

The applications menu is just one of the menus used by the Portfolio. The following description applies to not only this one, but all the menus on the Portfolio.

Selecting a Menu Item

You can select any menu item by just pressing the first letter of the item you require. So when the applications menu is displayed, to enter the Calculator press [C], or to enter the Diary, press [D].

You can also select a menu item by moving the cursor up or down to that item by pressing the [↑] or [↓] keys and then pressing [Return].

Escaping from a Menu

To return to the previous menu, whatever the current operation, press [Esc] (Escape).

When you use [Esc] to return to the previous menu, the cursor is always left on the selection you last used. So if you press [D] to select the Diary from the applications menu, when you press [Esc] to escape from the Diary back to the applications menu, the cursor is on the D of Diary.

The Screen Frame

When a menu is displayed on the screen on top of some other information, the previous menu or window is changed to a single-lined frame. The current menu or window is always a double-lined frame.

Dialogue Boxes

A special type of window is a *dialogue box*. This is a window (double-lined) which prompts you for some information - perhaps the name of a file. When you have typed the information, press [Return]. The information is then accepted by the Portfolio.

Sometimes a *default* value is offered in the dialogue box. That is a value which you might like to use. If this is not the value you want to use, either type a new one (the default will immediately be replaced by whatever you type) or use the cursor keys and the [Del/Ins] key to edit the default to the value you require.

Error Messages

Another special type of window is an *error message* window. If you type some inappropriate information - perhaps a file name with two dots instead of one (**file..old**), the Portfolio will respond by showing a window containing a message appropriate to the situation.

Note the details of the message and press any key to cancel the error and try again.

THE APPLICATIONS

The six programs available from the applications menu are:

The Address Book
The Calculator
The Diary
The Editor
The Setup Facility
The Worksheet

This section gives a brief description of the facilities of the programs. Refer to the following chapters for full details of the programs and their uses.

The Address Book

The Address Book is used to store all of your names, addresses and telephone numbers. When you have typed in a list of names, the Address Book can be used to search for a particular entry by typing the name, just part of the address or even part of the telephone number.

If you have a tone-dial telephone, you can use the Portfolio to auto-dial any number in the Address Book by pressing a single key.

The Address Book operates in two modes; Line mode, showing on the screen a list of names and telephone numbers, or Screen mode, showing the full name, number and address for a particular entry.

You can keep any number of Address Book files. For example, you might want to keep your home address file separate from your business address file. Or perhaps you might want a separate file for overseas contacts. You can organise the information any way you want.

You can create and edit Address Book files in the Editor (described below) and then load them into the Address Book, or you can create and edit the files directly from the Address Book itself.

The Calculator

The Portfolio Calculator operates in the same way as a desk-top calculator. The Calculator has five memories, a number of display modes (scientific, general, engineering and fixed decimal places), can print to a printer and produces factorials and square roots with a single key press.

The Calculator also has an editable 'tape'. As you perform a series of calculations, all parts of the calculations are shown on the screen and then scrolled upwards from the 'point of entry' onto the tape. You can then go back and change any part of the calculation by editing the tape and viewing the new results.

All output from the calculator may be printed via an optional communications adapter.

The Diary

The Portfolio Diary is a powerful appointments manager. It allows you to create and maintain any number of diaries for different purposes. The main diary may be used to set alarms on any appointments entered. Diary entries and alarms may be set to repeat daily, weekly, week-daily (non-week end), monthly or yearly.

Diary files can be searched for particular entries and entries can be moved from one date or time to another. The Portfolio Diary also operates in Calendar mode, allowing you to view the calendar for any date until the end of the year 2050!

The Editor

The Portfolio Editor is a text editor which allows you to type in documents. Documents are saved as plain-text files which can easily be transferred into your favourite word-processor on a desk-top pc.

The Editor has a powerful search and replace facility; may be set to word-wrap (or not) at any line length; allows documents to be merged together and can print via an optional communications adapter.

The Setup Facility

The Portfolio's Setup facility allows you to set a number of features of the computer so that it works best for your needs. You can change the way the display works; the use of sounds, the type of printer in use; the communications settings of an optional RS-232 port and a number of features of the application programs.

You can also use a built-in file transfer utility to transfer files to and from a desk-top pc.

The Worksheet

The Portfolio Worksheet is a powerful spreadsheet program which works like the industry-standard spreadsheet program, Lotus 1-2-3. Files created by the Worksheet can be read by Lotus 1-2-3 and, similarly, files created by Lotus 1-2-3 can be read by the Worksheet.

This means that you can produce a spreadsheet on your desk-top pc, transfer it to the Portfolio, and take your calculations everywhere you go.

For those who know a little about spreadsheet programs, the Worksheet allows you to use titles; insert and delete rows and columns; recalculate the sheet automatically or manually; flip between two windows on the sheet; set column widths; range paint and use a number of text and numeric formats including currency format.

The Worksheet grid is 127 columns wide by 255 rows deep.

3

THE COMMON FEATURES

The application programs built into the Portfolio share a number of features. This chapter describes those features in some detail. Where a feature described here is mentioned in other chapters, just a brief round-up is given.

It is recommended that you read this chapter before reading the chapters on the individual Portfolio applications.

THE KEYBOARD

The keyboard is used to type information into the Portfolio. There are 63 keys, laid out in the usual QWERTY fashion, although if you would like to use the French version (AZERTY) or the German version (QWERTZ), refer to the section on the Keyboard command in chapter 9.

The alphabetic keys, the numeric keys and the various punctuation keys need little or no introduction, but there are a few keys which offer more than just a simple character on the screen:

The [Return] Key

The [Return] key, the L shaped key at the right of the keyboard, is used to complete and confirm any action carried out on the Portfolio. Press [Return] at the end of a DOS command, at the end of an Address Book line, at the end of a calculation in the Calculator, at the end of a Diary entry, at the end of a paragraph in the Editor and at the end of a cell's contents in the Worksheet.

The Cursor Keys

The cursor is the flashing block on the Portfolio's screen which shows where your next typed input will appear. The cursor keys ([↑], [↓], [→], [←]) are found at the lower right corner of the keyboard. The cursor keys are used to move the cursor up, down, right or left.

The cursor keys can also be used in conjunction with the [Ctrl] and [Fn] keys in the application programs. These keys combinations, which are all described fully in the following chapters, allow you to move the cursor around the current file by a word or a page at a time.

The [Esc] Key

The [Esc] (Escape) key at the top left of the keyboard is used to escape from the current activity in any of the application programs on the Portfolio. If you think you have made an error, or you want to escape from a command or a menu, press [Esc]. (If you are using DOS, hold down the [Ctrl] key and press [C] to cancel an operation.)

The [Shift] Keys

The [Shift] keys (marked ⇑), at the ends of the second row up, are used like the shift key on a typewriter. They allow you to type upper or lower case letters, and a second range of punctuation marks as shown on the keys.

The [BS] Key

The [BS] (BackSpace) key at the top right of the keyboard is used to back up through any typed information, deleting characters as you go (when the keyboard is in Insert mode) or just to back up through typed information, changing and deleting nothing (Overtype mode). See the following description of the [Del/Ins] key.

The [Del/Ins] Key

The [Del/Ins] (Delete/Insert) key, as the name suggests, has two functions; to delete the character beneath the cursor and (with the [Shift] key) to set the keyboard into Insert mode.

Insert & Overtype Mode

When typing information into the Portfolio, the keyboard can operate in either of two modes; Insert mode or Overtype mode. The names suggest how the two modes work. When the keyboard is in Overtype mode, anything you type characters overwrites any text already shown on the screen at the cursor position. When the keyboard is in Insert mode, the new characters are inserted at the current position, and any characters in the way are pushed across to the right.

This means that you have two ways of editing information on the Portfolio, by inserting and by overtyping. You can use whichever mode you find most comfortable when typing and editing information.

When you first use the Portfolio, the keyboard is in Overtype mode. To change to Insert mode, hold down the [Shift] key and press [Del/Ins]. To change back to Overtype mode, press the same keys again.

The [Lock] Key

The [Lock] key, at the left end of the middle row, is used together with other keys to set the keyboard into Caps mode (Caps Lock), Numeric mode (Num Lock) or Scroll Lock mode as follows:

- Hold down [Shift] and press [Lock] for Caps mode
- Hold down [/I\] and press [Lock] for Numeric mode
- Hold down [Fn] and press [Lock] for Scroll Lock mode.

The [Lock] key can also be used in the applications, when the screen frame has been removed with [F5], to see the date, time and keyboard status. Just press [Lock], the status line is shown at the bottom of the screen, then release.

The [/I\] Key

The [/I\] key, at the lower left hand corner of the keyboard, is a special key whose uses are unique to the Portfolio. It is used to start the application programs built into the Portfolio, to use the numeric keypad (see below) and to alter the Portfolio's screen contrast.

Using the [/|\] key to start the application programs is described in chapter 2. Using the [/|\] key to alter the screen contrast is described in chapter 1.

The [/|\] key allows access to the following characters and facilities:

The [Fn] Key

The [Fn] (Function) key is used to turn the numeric keys along the top of the keyboard into Function keys. It is also used with the cursor keys to move the cursor very rapidly around files.

The [Fn] key also has a number of other uses, including setting the keyboard into different modes, as follows:

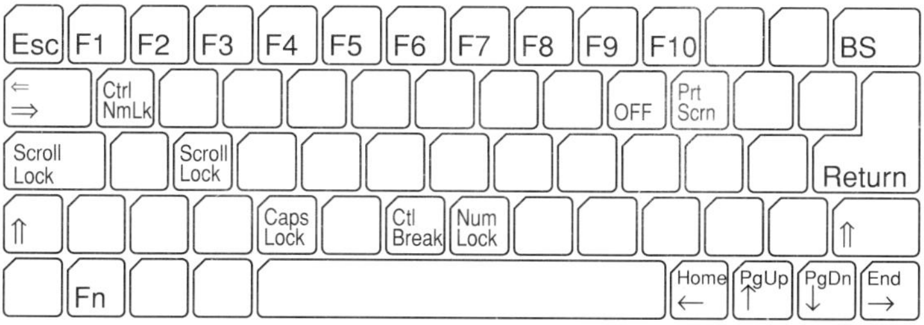

[Fn] [←]	[Home] Key
[Fn] [→]	[End] Key
[Fn] [↑]	[Pg Up] Key
[Fn] [↓]	[Pg Dn] Key
[Fn] [B]	Break
[Fn] [C]	Caps Lock
[Fn] [N]	Numeric mode
[Fn] [O]	Switch Portfolio to standby mode (Off)
[Fn] [P]	Print Screen
[Fn] [Q]	[Ctrl NumLock] Key
[Fn] [S]	Scroll Lock

Using Function Keys

The function keys, on a desk-top pc and on the Portfolio, are used to perform a range of operations with a single keypress. All of the function key operations are described in detail in the relevant chapters in this book.

The function keys are numbered 1 to 10, and are described in this book as [F1], [F2] and so on. When you need to type [F1], hold down the [Fn] key and press [1].

The function keys [F1] to [F5] have the same effect in all of the application programs as follows:

[F1]	Display the current application command menu
[F2]	Request help
[F3]	Display the Clipboard menu
[F4]	Undo the most previous delete operation, at the current cursor position
[F5]	Zoom the screen frame on or off.

The uses of function keys [F6] to [F10] in the application programs are described in detail in the relevant chapters in this book.

The Numeric Keypad

When typing a lot of numbers, perhaps in the Editor or the Worksheet, it is easier to use the sort of keypad found on a calculator, with all of the numbers and the arithmetic signs grouped together. Computers have their numbers spread along the top line of the keyboard, and the arithmetic signs almost as widely spread. The Portfolio avoids this problem by having a 'buried' numeric keypad, marked in magenta, to the right of the keyboard.

To use the numeric keypad, along with the arithmetic signs, hold down the [Fn] key and press the [N] key; this puts the keyboard into Numeric mode. Now you can use the numeric keypad just like using a calculator keypad.

To return the keyboard to Normal mode, again hold down the [Fn] key and press [N].

When you use the Portfolio Calculator, the keyboard is automatically set in Numeric mode and automatically returns to Normal mode when you leave the Calculator.

The [Ctrl] Key

The [Ctrl] (Control) key, when used with various letter keys on the keyboard, allows you to perform a variety of operations either in DOS or in the application programs with a single keypress. All of the [Ctrl] key operations are described in detail in the relevant chapters in this book.

The [Alt] Key

The [Alt] key, at the left hand end of the space bar, is used on the Portfolio to gain access to a number of special characters which are not ordinarily available from the keyboard.

Firstly, the following characters can be typed. Hold down [Alt] and press the following keys:

- [[ ] gives **£**
- [ ]] gives ~
- ['] gives '

In addition to these three characters, you can gain access to any of the 224 printable characters shown in the table in appendix A. To access any character, first set the keyboard into Numeric mode; hold down the [/|\] key and press [Lock]; now hold down the [Alt] key, type on the numeric keypad the ASCII code for the required character and release the [Alt] key. The character appears on the screen.

For example, you might want to insert the Æ character (ASCII character 146) at the start of the word Æsop in a document:

- Hold down the [/|\] key and press [Lock]
- Hold down the [Alt] key and type 146 on the numeric keypad
- Release the [Alt] key; the character appears at the cursor position.

You can now set the keyboard into Normal mode (hold down the [/|\] key and press [Lock]) to continue typing.

THE APPLICATION PROGRAMS

In addition to using the function keys as mentioned above, the application programs use various key presses and key combinations for particular operations. These key presses are described here. For further detail on any application program, refer to the relevant chapter in this book.

Key Press	Action
[Ctrl] [A]	Go to start of current file
[Ctrl] [B]	Delete back to start of line
[Ctrl] [D]	Redial telephone number (Address Book)
[Ctrl] [E]	Delete to end of line
[E]	Exponent (Calculator)
[Ctrl] [L]	Delete whole of current line
[Ctrl] [R]	Replace text (Editor)
[Ctrl] [S]	Search for text (Editor)
[Ctrl] [U]	Return to previous cursor position
[Ctrl] [W]	Delete word to right of cursor
[Ctrl] [Z]	Go to end of current file
[Ctrl] [BS]	Delete word to left of cursor
[Ctrl] [→]	Move cursor one word to right
[Ctrl] [←]	Move cursor one word to left
[Fn] [←]	Go to start of current line
	Go to today (Diary)
	Go to cell A1 (Worksheet)
[Fn] [→]	Go to end of current line
[Tab]	Insert new record (Address Book)
	Change sign (Calculator)
	Move cursor one screen to right (Worksheet)
[Space]	Clear entry (Calculator)

[Return]	Change from Line to Screen mode (Address Book)
	Change from Calendar to Diary mode (Diary)
[Esc]	Change from Screen to Line mode (Address Book)
	Change from Diary to Calendar mode (Diary)
	Escape from menu or activity (all applications).

PC KEYS ON THE PORTFOLIO

If you are used to using a desk-top pc keyboard, the following list shows how to access certain keys on the Portfolio:

Desk-top pc	Portfolio
[Prt Sc]	[Fn] [P]
[Pg Up]	[Fn] [↑]
[Pg Dn]	[Fn] [↓]
[Home]	[Fn] [←]
[End]	[Fn] [→]
[Caps Lock]	[Fn] [C]
[Num Lock]	[Fn] [N]
[Scrl Lock]	[Fn] [S]
[Caps Lock]	[Fn] [C]
[Insert]	[Shift] [Del/Ins]
[Delete]	[Del/Ins]
[Ctrl Break]	[Fn] [B]

[£]	[Alt] [{]
[~]	[Alt] [}]
[‘]	[Alt] [’]

FILE HANDLING

The four application programs which use files to store information; the Address Book, Diary, Editor and Worksheet, all deal with files in the same way.

When you run any of these application programs, press [F1] to see the application's command menu. The first item in the menu is **Files**. This option leads to a further menu containing options concerned with handling files. The **Files** menu looks like this:

Note that the **Merge** option does not appear in the Worksheet's **Files** menu, and that the Address Book has an additional item, **Write Selected** (see below).

Loading & Saving

Before we look in detail at what the **Files** menu options can do for us, a few general words on loading and saving are called for. As we saw in chapter 2, the file-based applications store information on either the RAM drive or a memory card in the form of files.

The files can be stored all at the same level, in the **root level directory**, or you might like to create a directory and store files there. The use of directories is described in detail in chapter 2 and in chapter 4 under the description of the DOS command **md** (Make Directory).

When you start an application program, for example, the Worksheet, the grid is blank and the Portfolio automatically gives the new, blank file the name **unnamed.wks** (displayed on the top line of the screen frame). This is just a general name used by all of the applications to show that a new, blank file has been started. The other application programs add their own default file extensions (Address Book - **unnamed.adr**; Diary - **unnamed.dry**; Editor - **unnamed.txt**).

You can now either load a file from one of the drives, or you can start typing in information at the keyboard. If you load a file from a drive, the name of the file is then displayed on the upper edge of the screen frame. If you start typing information at the keyboard, the name **unnamed.wks** remains.

When you want to save the information in the current file, you are advised to save the file under a name appropriate to the information in the file and not to use unnamed.wks.

Then when you next use the Worksheet, or when you use the **Files: New** command described below, the file name **unnamed.wks** can again be safely used by the Portfolio to denote a new, blank file.

THE GOLDEN RULE

The Golden Rule when using any type of computer is this - and there are no exceptions:

- **Always make a back-up copy of any file which is really important.**

You can make a copy onto a memory card or via the optional communications link to a desk-top pc. Then if disaster strikes, you have a copy of your important data.

THE FILES COMMANDS

The Files: New Command

If you have made any changes to the current file since it was last saved, the file changed symbol will be shown at the upper right corner of the screen frame. If you then select the **Files: New** command, the Portfolio prompts you to save the file, complete with its changes. The screen shows:

```
Save Current?
Yes
No
```

Note that if you select Yes, the file is saved under the name shown on the top line of the screen frame, even if the current file name is **unnamed.xxx**. The current file name is then reset by the Portfolio to **unnamed.xxx**. If you then save the new, blank file under the name **unnamed.xxx**, the previous version of the file, with the changes you made, will be lost. You should always make sure that when you save your current file, the file name is one **you** have chosen, rather than **unnamed.xxx**. To save the file under a new name, you should use the **Files: Save as** command described below.

If you select **No**, the changes made to the current file are discarded and the file name is automatically reset to **unnamed.xxx**.

The Files: Load Command

The **Files: Load** command is used to load an existing file from a drive into an application. A copy of the file is made from the original which is stored on the drive - loading a file does not have any effect on the original file, unlike saving (see the **Files: Save as** command below).

When you select the **Files: Load** command, the Portfolio prompts you to enter the name of the file you want to load. The screen shows, for example:

```
═══════════ Load ═══════════
 Name: C:\SHEETS\UNNAMED.WKS
```

All of the **Files** commands which deal with files on drives (**Load**, **Save as**, **Print**, **Merge** and **Write Selected**) operate in basically the same way via a dialogue box like that shown above. The dialogue box is used to prompt for the name of a file. There are a number of ways of specifying a particular file, and the Portfolio always offers you a default file name in the dialogue box.

The default file name is always the file name most recently used by the current application program. If the current file name is, for example, **unnamed.wks**, that is the file name offered by the dialogue box. You now have four options from which to choose:

1. Press [Return] to load the file shown in the dialogue box

If you have loaded a file, edited the file and then wish to return to the original file, as it was before you made the changes, press [Return] when the file name is offered.

2. Edit the file name to that of the file you want to load

If the default file name in the box is, for example, **unnamed.wks**, and you want to load a file called **vat1.wks**, you can move the cursor to the appropriate part of the file name in the dialogue box and change the name offered until it shows the name you need, then press [Return].

3. Press the [*] key

The [*] key calls up a list of all files with the default file extension for the current application, in the current directory. The files are listed in the form of a menu, from which you can make a selection in the usual way. When you select a file, that file is loaded into memory.

Note that pressing [*] is the equivalent of typing ***.*** (see chapter 4 for more details of this in relation to DOS). You can also type a full path name with or without a file name, including wildcards, just like those used in DOS.

4. Press the [:] key to see a list of all of the files and subdirectories found in the current directory.

The files are listed in the form of a menu, from which you can make a selection in the usual way. If the current directory is not the root level directory (see chapter 2 and 4), the parent directory and any sub-directories appear at the start of the list. For example, if the current directory is **c:\sheets**, in which there is a sub-directory called **sales**, and two worksheets, the screen would show:

```
C:\SHEETS\*.*
..              <DIR>
SALES           <DIR>
MAR90.WKS
APR90.WKS
```

You can select either of the Worksheet files in the usual way, or select the parent directory or sub-directory. If you select either of the directories, another list is displayed of all of the files in the directory chosen, from which you can again make a selection.

The Files: Save as Command

The **Files: Save as** command is used to save a copy of the current file under the same or a different name on any drive. If there is already a copy of the file under the name you use, **the old copy will be overwritten by the new copy**, so make sure you are not losing some vital information by using an existing file name.

If you save a new copy of a file under a different name to the file originally loaded, then the original file will be unaffected when you make your new copy.

For full details of the way in which file names are given, refer to the section above under the heading **Files: Load**.

The Files: Merge Command

The **Merge** command allows you to load a file into the Address Book, the Diary or the Editor without first discarding the current file (if any); the new file is merged with the current file to make a new, larger file.

For full details of the way in which file names are given, refer to the section above under the heading **Files: Load**.

When **Merge** is used in the Address book, the two files are merged together and then alphabetically sorted, so the new file appears just like an Address Book file which has been created in the usual way.

When **Merge** is used in the Diary, the two files are merged together and then sorted by date and time, so the new file appears just like a Diary file which has been created in the usual way.

When **Merge** is used in the Editor, the file specified is inserted into the current file at the position of the cursor. For example, to add the contents of another file to the end of the current file, you should position the cursor at the end of the current file before selecting **Merge**.

After using the **Merge** command, remember that if you want to keep a copy of the new, merged file, use the **Save as** command in the **Files** menu to make a new copy of the combined file.

The Files: Print Command

The **Print** command is used to print the contents of the current file to a printer (serial or parallel) or to a file on a drive. For more information on the destination of your printed output, see the section under the heading PREPARING TO PRINT in chapter 9. For more information on the format of the your printed output, see the relevant chapters on each of the application programs.

The Files: Write Selected Command

One of the facilities of the Address Book allows you to select a number of the records in the current Address Book file according to certain criteria. For example, you might want to select all of the records which feature the dialling code 010.

Having made this selection, you might want to save this sub-set of the current file as a separate, smaller file, perhaps with the name **overseas.adr**. The **Write Selected** command, which appears only in the **Files** menu in the Address Book, allows you to do so. Having saved a sub-set of the current file under a new name, the original file is unaffected by the operation and is intact on the original drive.

For full details of the way in which file names are given, refer to the section above under the heading **Files: Load**. For more information on the use of the Address Book, see chapter 5.

HELP!

Don't worry, help is on hand. Whatever you are doing, you can always ask the Portfolio for help. There are two built-in help systems which offer advice and reminders on the menus, the function keys, keyboard short-cuts and a range of other topics.

General Help

When you are using any of the applications except Setup, you can call for general help by pressing [F2]. The screen shows the general **Help** menu:

```
Help
Keyboard
Clipboard
Undelete
Function Keys
```

This menu offers help on the four topics shown; the keyboard, the clipboard, undeleting information and the function keys.

Specific Help

More help is available from within each application by referring to the **Help** command in the application's main command menu (press [F1]). This help is described in detail in the chapters on the application programs, later in this book.

THE CLIPBOARD

The clipboard is an area of memory which can be used to to hold a block of information from any file, ready to be pasted into some other part of the same file, or even another file.

The information might be a few lines from a document, a record from the Address Book, a few entries from the Diary, even a block of cells from a Worksheet file. The only limit to the amount of information put into the clipboard is the amount of free memory in the Portfolio.

You can even transfer information between the different applications by using the clipboard. You can type in a number of lines of text in the Editor, cut or copy them into the clipboard and then paste the whole block into the Address Book, the Diary or the Worksheet. See also chapter 15 on The Application File Formats.

The process of using the clipboard is very simple; you move to the start of the required block of information and mark the start. You then move to the end of the block and either cut the block or copy the block into the clipboard. The information then remains in the clipboard, ready to be pasted into a new position or a new file, any number of times.

The clipboard is operated from within The Address Book, Diary, Editor or Worksheet, by pressing [F3]. The screen then shows the clipboard menu:

```
Clipboard
Cut
Store
Paste
Mark
```

Clipboard: Mark

The **Mark** option is used to mark the start of the block of information. Position the cursor at the start of the block and select **Mark**. There is no visible mark, but the Portfolio remembers the place.

Clipboard: Store

The **Store** option is used to make a copy of all information between the start mark and the current cursor position. The information is not cut from the current file - just a copy is taken and placed in the clipboard.

Clipboard: Cut

The **Cut** option is used to cut out of the current file all information between the start mark and the current cursor position. The information is all stored in the clipboard. To replace the block of information in the same position, just press [F3] to view the clipboard menu again and press [P] to paste the block straight back.

Clipboard: Paste

The **Paste** option is used to paste a copy of the entire contents of the clipboard into the current file at the current cursor position. The information can be copied from the clipboard into any number of files any number of times (provided you have enough free memory in the Portfolio).

The Clipboard File

When you copy or cut information into the clipboard, the information is stored by the Portfolio in a file called **clipbord.dat** in the directory **\system** (see chapters 2 and 4 for more information on files and directories).

You can also choose to either keep the clipboard when you escape from the applications menu or to discard it. See the description of the Clipboard Save facility within Setup (chapter 9). The Portfolio automatically keeps the clipboard file when you leave the applications menu. To empty the clipboard, you can either delete the clipboard file from DOS by typing:

```
del \system\clipbord.dat [Return]
```

or from within an application:

- Press [F3] to see the clipboard menu
- Press [M] to select **Mark**
- Press [F3] to see the clipboard menu
- Press [S] to store everything back to the mark (in this case nothing).

DELETING & UNDELETING

Every time you delete a character or a word or a line or a cell of information in the applications, it is saved in a file called undelete.dat, rather like the clipboard file described above. The only limit to the amount of information put into the undelete file is the amount of free memory in the Portfolio.

All information deleted in any way (other than by the clipboard's Cut option) can then later be undeleted by pressing [F4].

For example, you might be using the Address Book and decide to delete an entry, so in Line mode you move to the entry and press the [Del/Ins] key. The entry is then stored in the undelete file. You might then go into a Worksheet file, type some new figures and delete some old ones - pressing [Del/Ins] deletes the contents of the cell at the cursor position.

You could now go into the Editor, start a new file and press [F4] a number of times. Each press of [F4] undeletes the most recent deletion, placing it at the cursor position, just as if it had been retyped. It is also then removed from the undelete file. If you press [F4] enough times, the undelete file will eventually be emptied - no further information can then be undeleted.

The whole undelete process is like a stack of books on a table; as you remove books from your bookshelves, you put them onto the pile. Then later on you take them off the pile a put them somewhere else (or back in the same position), and the height of the pile goes down until it is empty - you can't replace books that are not in the pile.

You can also choose to either keep the undelete file when you escape from the applications menu or to discard it. See the description of the Undelete Save facility within Setup (chapter 9). The Portfolio automatically keeps the undelete file when you leave the applications menu. To empty the undelete file, you just delete the file itself from DOS by typing:

```
del \system\undelete.dat [Return]
```

4

THE OPERATING SYSTEM

WHAT IS DOS?

DOS stands for *Disk Operating System*, from the days when all computers used magnetic disks to store information. DOS is a program which the Portfolio uses to organise its every operation. DOS is used as a filing system, as a way of putting information on the screen, as a way of reading key-presses from the keyboard, as a way of sending information to a printer and as a way of making other programs run.

So much for what DOS does for the Portfolio, but what can DOS do for YOU? A great deal; you can think of DOS as your servant. You tell DOS to do something, and away it goes on the errand. But this servant, although very intelligent and powerful, takes every command very literally. It will do exactly as you tell it, no more - no less.

For example, you might have a letter in the Portfolio which you have just typed: You want a copy of the letter to be made on a memory card, so you tell DOS to make the copy; you want to delete the original copy of the letter from the Portfolio's memory, so you tell DOS to delete the file; you want to see what files are in the Portfolio's memory and then examine the contents of one of them, so you ask DOS for a list of files and tell it to show the contents of one file on the screen.

This chapter describes how the Portfolio stores information and how you to make the most of DOS as a filing system. This chapter also includes a full reference on all of the commands available in DOS.

Some of the DOS commands will be useful on a day to day basis; others will only rarely be used. Don't feel that you must plough through the reference section, absorbing everything, for now, just read the HOW INFORMATION IS STORED section. However, a few of the commands are worth reading about quite soon:

The **copy** command	Used to copy one or more files from one place to another or to make new copies under different names
The **dir** command	Used to read the directory of files on a drive
The **del** command	Used to delete one or more files which are no longer required
The **md** command	Used to make a new directory for storing files
The **rd** command	Used to remove an empty directory
The **cd** command	Used to change from one directory to another.

These are just a few of the more simple things that DOS can do for you. You might like to read the descriptions of these commands before getting to grips with the chapters on the application programs later in the book. But first, let's take a look at how how DOS stores information.

HOW INFORMATION IS STORED

The application programs built into the Portfolio store information in the computer's memory in the form of *files*.

What is a File?

A computer file is rather like a card file you slip into a filing cabinet. It is a self-contained unit and contains information on a particular subject. It might be the minutes from a meeting or a list of all the company's employees.

If you want to start a new file for new subject, just like taking a new clean card folder, the Portfolio allows you to do so. Similarly, if the information in a file becomes out of date or no longer wanted, the whole file can simply and quickly be deleted.

However, once a file has been deleted, it has then gone for good! A file should only be deleted when you are sure you no longer need its contents.

File Names

Each file stored in the Portfolio is given a *file name*. A file name may be up to eight characters long. File names can consist of letters or numbers or a mixture, for example:

```
letter1        employmt
job-25-3       bankletr
```

Notice that the files are given names which are relevant to their contents. If you use filenames like 0001, 0002, 0003 and so on, you might get a little confused when looking for the file containing a letter to your bank manager. So choose names which reflect the contents of the files in question - it makes life much easier later on.

Also, if you write a lot of letters to the bank, it makes sense to give the files similar names, perhaps **bnkaug01** (bank: August 1), **bnkaug02** (bank: August 2), **bnksep01** (bank: September 1) and so on. This means that you can refer to groups of files whose names start with the same letters. More on this topic later.

As an extra guide to the contents of a particular file, you can also add a *file extension*. A file extension may consist of up to three letters and numbers and is separated from the file name by a dot (.). The application programs add their own file extensions automatically as follows:

Address Book files	**.adr**
Diary files	**.dry**
Editor files	**.txt**
Worksheet files	**.wks**

For example:

```
letter1.txt      costs.wks
address.adr      home.adr
diary.dry        business.dry
```

You can create files in a variety of ways which have different file extensions to these, but the applications always use these extensions unless you specify otherwise.

Illegal File Names

There are number of file names which DOS reserves for its own use and which you should not attempt to use. These are:

```
aux, clock$, com, con, lpt, nul, prn
```

These names, with the exception of **clock$**, may be used as file extensions, but not as file names. More details are given on these special names later in this chapter under the heading DEVICE NAMES.

Directories

When you are storing your card files in a filing cabinet, you might also organise them in larger groups in the separate drawers of the cabinet. For example, the top drawer might be used for all of your letters, the middle drawer for the accounts and the bottom drawer for your employment and personnel records.

In just the same way, you can organise the files in the Portfolio's memory into *directories*. A directory is just like a drawer in a filing cabinet: it can hold a large number of files, it organises your storage space and makes finding a particular file much easier.

Each directory has a *directory name* which may consist of up to eight letters and numbers, and can have an extension like an ordinary file.

The advantage of the Portfolio over a filing cabinet is that you can have as many directories (drawers) as you like, you can add another directory at any time, you can remove directories and you can have directories within directories! A directory within a directory is called a *sub-directory*.

The Portfolio's internal memory, where the directories are created, is in fact a directory itself, but this one is special. This directory, referred to as the *root level directory*, does not have a normal directory name and it cannot be removed. The Portfolio allows you to have as many directories as you like in the root level directory and also a large number of ordinary files - just like any other directory.

Let's take the example of a single file; a letter to the bank. The text of the letter is in a file called **bnkaug01.txt**. The file is in a directory called **\banklet** which is stored at the root level directory.

The Portfolio's Drives

To complete our knowledge of how the Portfolio organises files, we must know about *drives*. The name comes from when all computers had disk drives - into which were placed floppy disks. Each disk drive was given a letter, a, b, c and so on. The Portfolio has drives too, but it has no disks.

The word drive now refers to an area of the Portfolio's memory which acts like a disk drive as described above. Directories and files are created on this drive, which can be written to and read just like a disk drive on a desk-top computer. The internal drive, also called a *RAM drive* (because it is made up of RAM; *Random Access Memory*), is referred to as **c:**.

The Portfolio also has another drive, the slot at the left hand side of the computer. This is a *memory card drive*; instead of a disk, you use a *memory card* to store information.

There is always a *current drive*, that is the drive on which DOS commands will automatically be carried out (unless you specify otherwise). The current drive is sometimes known as the *default drive*.

When typing drive specifiers, path names and file names, you may use upper or lower case letters or a mixture of the two.

Paths & Path Names

A path might be thought of as the path to a file. This may include a a directory and sub-directory, although it may just be a single directory. For example:

```
\sales\figures
\sales
```

A path name is a path plus a file name, for example:

```
\sales\figures\costs.wks
\sales\letter1.txt
```

Using Wildcards

When you want to carry out an operation on a particular file, you must give the full file name. However, sometimes, you might want to look at a group of files with similar names. For example, you might want to see a list of files which all have the extension **.wks**.

You can use two *wildcards* when specifying file names, * and **?**. The first, *, stands for any group of characters in a file name or extension and the second, **?** stands for any single character.

Using the example above, you might want to see a list of the files with the extension **.wks**, so, using the DOS command **dir** (directory), you type:

```
dir *.wks [Return]
```

The command says, 'show a list of all files in the default directory which have the extension **.wks**'.

If you have transferred Lotus 1-2-3 files from a desk-top pc, some of the files might have the extension **.wk1**. In this case, you would type:

```
dir *.wk? [Return]
```

Another example; you have a number of files which have three letter file names. You want to see a list of these, but not the longer file names. You would type:

```
dir ???.* [Return]
```

However, this would also display file names with only one or two letters in the file name.

Memory Cards

Memory cards, like the Portfolio's RAM drive, are solid-state devices, they have no moving parts. When a memory card is plugged into the Portfolio's memory card drive, the card can be used to store information in exactly the same way as in the RAM drive - but the card can be removed.

This means that you can use different cards for different purposes. You can organise your files in whatever way suits you best. Memory cards are available in a variety of capacities, and come with full instructions.

The Portfolio's memory card drive is referred to as drive **a:**. The letter used to refer to a drive (**a:**, **b:** and so on) is called the *drive designator.*

Apart from the drive designator, which refers to the drive itself, not the card which is used in the drive, the card itself can also be given a name, a *volume name*. A volume name is used to distinguish between one card and another. More details of volume labels are given under the descriptions of the DOS commands **vol** and **label**, later in this chapter.

The Golden Rule

The Golden Rule when using any type of computer is this - and there are no exceptions:

- **Always make a back-up copy of any file which is really important.**

You can make a copy onto a memory card or via the optional communications link to a desk-top pc. Then if disaster strikes, you have a copy of your important data.

The RAM Drive

The Portfolio's RAM drive is a special sort of drive, because really it is just an area of the Portfolio's memory. The computer's memory is used to run programs, to hold the information in files you are currently working on and part of it is used as a RAM drive.

The area of memory used as a RAM drive is set aside automatically the first time you use the Portfolio, you don't have to do a thing. This means that you always have a drive where you can save information, and this drive is **c:**.

However, if you keep on saving information in files on **c:**, it will eventually become full. The Portfolio will still be able to operate, but you will not be able to save any more files on **c:**. You should therefore take care to delete any unwanted information from **c:** so that this doesn't happen.

If you feel that the RAM drive should be made bigger - taking up a greater proportion of the Portfolio's memory and giving you more storage space, you can change the size with the DOS command **fdisk**. This command is described in detail later in this chapter.

THE DOS PROMPT

We now know some of the things DOS can do for us, but what is it? How can I see it? What does it look like?

DOS shows itself to us as a *prompt*; a few characters at the left hand side of the screen with a flashing *cursor* - a block which shows us where on the screen our typed commands will appear.

When you first switch on the Portfolio, the prompt looks like this:

```
c>
```

This shows that the current drive is **c:** and that you can now enter a DOS command.

There is a DOS command, **prompt**, which allows you to change the prompt which DOS displays on the screen. For example, you could change it to 'Hello Jo' or, more usefully, change it to show the current time and the current drive. For more details of the **prompt** command, see the description of that command later in this chapter.

IN THE BEGINNING...

When you first start up the Portfolio, a directory called **\system** is created on drive **c:**. In this directory the Portfolio stores a file called **permdata.dat** and two more files called **clipbord.dat** and **undelete.dat**.

The last two of these files may or may not appear, according to two settings made in the Setup facility. See chapter 9 for full details of these files.

The file **permdata.dat** is used by the Portfolio to store information on how you use the computer; whether the screen frame should be displayed in each of the applications, the most recent file names used and so on. You should leave this file in place, unless you want to reset the Portfolio's applications to the way they were when you first used the computer.

AUTOEXEC.BAT & CONFIG.SYS

These two horrific file names actually make sense when you know what the files contain. Let's look at them in turn.

Autoexec.bat

When you switch on a desk-top pc, the computer searches all of its drives for a file called **autoexec.bat**. This is a batch file (hence the extension) which is automatically executed whenever the computer is switched on (hence the same).

The file typically contains commands which change the DOS prompt or automatically run a program. You should read the section at the end of this chapter on BATCH FILES. Briefly though, they are plain text files (you can create them in the Portfolio's Editor) which contain a number of DOS commands.

The **autoexec.bat** file is only run on the Portfolio when you press [Ctrl] [Alt] [Del/Ins] to reset the computer, or when you type:

```
autoexec [Return]
```

Config.sys

The **config.sys** file is used by the Portfolio to store a number of system configuration settings (hence the name). This file is a plain-text file (which can also be created in the Portfolio's Editor) which can contain any of these commands:

buffers=nn	Where nn is any number up to 64. The recommended value is 32. This sets the size of the disk cache buffer. Don't worry about what this means it is just part of the Portfolio's way of reading and writing information to the drives
files=nn	Where nn is any number up to 20 (the recommended value). This number sets the maximum number of files the Portfolio can open at one time. You can only ever open one file at a time, but the Portfolio

	may open more purely for its own use while you are working
country=nnn	Where nnn is a three digit number from the list below. The number should be the one alongside your country. The Portfolio uses this setting when deciding, among other things, which date format to use (mm/dd/yy or dd/mm/yy)
device=<x>	Where <x> is the name of a device driver, such as **ansi.sys**
break=on/off	Allows DOS to check for the break key ([Fn] [B]) more frequently. The break key causes the Portfolio to stop its current activity. Initially, break is off. If you press the break key when break is off, the Portfolio will stop its current activity during input from the keyboard or output to the screen. If you press the break key when break is on, the Portfolio will also stop its current activity during certain drive operations.
shell=<x>	Where <x> is a command shell such as **command.com**. The file **command.com** is used on desk-top pc's instead of the ROM based command interpreter in the Portfolio, but it would be possible to transfer such a file into the Portfolio, and install it using this command in the **config.sys** file.

The following list shows the country codes for use with the **country** command described above:

Country	**nnn**	**Date format**
Australia	061	dd/mm/yy
Belgium	032	dd/mm/yy

Denmark	045	dd/mm/yy
Finland	358	dd/mm/yy
France	033	dd/mm/yy
Germany	049	dd/mm/yy
Italy	039	dd/mm/yy
Netherlands	031	dd/mm/yy
Norway	047	dd/mm/yy
Spain	034	dd/mm/yy
Sweden	046	yy/mm/dd
Switzerland	041	dd/mm/yy
UK	044	dd/mm/yy
USA	001	mm/dd/yy

So, it is recommended that later on, when you have read the chapter on the Editor, you create a file called **config.sys** and enter the first three of the commands described above, each on a separate line. Save the file in the root level directory. The file might read:

```
buffers=32
files=20
country=044
```

DEVICE NAMES

Earlier in this chapter is a list of file names which DOS reserves for its own use. The correct name for these special names is *device names* and they are as follows:

aux	An auxiliary input device, perhaps an RS-232 port
clock$	The internally stored clock/calendar
com	The RS-232 port

con	The console (keyboard and screen)
lpt	The parallel printer port
nul	A null device
prn	The printer.

More details of the uses for these device names are given under the descriptions of individual DOS commands later in this chapter.

THE FUNCTION KEYS

After typing a DOS command, if you need to then type a similar command, you can use the function keys to recall all or part of the previous command.

When you type a DOS command and press [Return], a copy of the command is stored by DOS. This is called the **template**. By using the function keys you can perform the following:

Function Key	Effect
[F1]	Copies one character from the template to the command line. Further presses of [F1] copy subsequent characters from the template onto the command line, until the whole template has been copied
[F2] x	Copies characters up the specified character (shown here by the letter x) from the template onto the command line
[F3]	Copies the remainder of the template onto the command line
[F4] x	Skips over all characters in the template up to the specified character (shown here by the letter x)

[F5]	Copies a new command line into the template (before [Return] is pressed) but does not execute the command line
[F6]	Places a CONTROL Z character (End of File) at the end of the new template
[Del/Ins]	Skips over one character in the template
[Esc]	Abandons the current command line
[Shift][Del/Ins]	Allows characters to be inserted in the template.

Those descriptions of using the function keys may seem awfully complicated, so the best thing you can do is experiment. Try a simple DOS command like:

```
dir /p [Return]
```

A list of the files in the current directory is displayed on the screen a page at a time. Now try pressing [F1] a few times, until the whole command reappears. Now press [F3] and the whole command will reappear in one. Now you begin to see how the function keys can help.

Using the function keys becomes really helpful if you have to type a very long DOS command, or one which contains long and awkward filenames.

For example, you want to copy the file **dfj1g555.txt** to a file called **david.txt**. You type the command:

```
copy dfjig555.txt david.txt [Return]
```

But DOS presents the message **File not found**. Then you realise you have used an i in the middle of the filename instead of a 1. To recall the command from the template up to the i, type:

```
[F2] i 1 [F3]
```

The command is now shown on the screen correctly, press [Return] to execute the command. So instead of retyping the whole 27 key command - with the possibility of making a different mistake - you only had to press 4 keys to correct the command.

The [Ctrl] Key

In addition to using the function keys as described above, the [Ctrl] key gives you the following facilities:

[Ctrl] [C]	aborts current process and returns to the DOS prompt
[Ctrl] [P]	toggle output to printer. This switch causes all screen output from DOS to also be sent to a printer. See the chapter on the Setup facility for details of getting ready to use a printer
[Ctrl] [S]	pause screen output; press any key to continue.

THE DOS COMMANDS

This section includes a list of all of the DOS commands used on the Portfolio, followed by a detailed explanation of each of the commands. DOS commands, drive specifiers, path names and file names may all be typed in upper or lower case letters or a mixture of the two:

app	Start application programs
break	Enable/Disable DOS break facility
cd (chdir)	Change to another directory
chkdsk	Check drive status
cls	Clear the Portfolio's screen
copy	Copy one or more files
date	Set the date in the internal clock/calendar
del	Delete one or more files

dir	Read the directory (list of files) on a drive
echo	Switch on/off output of batch commands to screen
@echo	As echo but without displaying ECHO command
errorlevel	Tests a batch file exit code
fdisk	Reset the size of the RAM drive
for/in/do	Looping command structure
format	Format a memory card
help	List all DOS commands
goto	Batch file redirection structure
if	Batch file conditional structure
label	Write a new volume label to the RAM drive or a memory card
md (mkdir)	Make a new directory
off	Switch the Portfolio into standby mode
pause	Pauses batch file execution
path	Set a new DOS search path
prompt	Set a new DOS prompt
rd (rmdir)	Remove a directory
rem	REMark in a batch file
ren	Rename one or more files
run	Run a program from a memory card
set	Set or read the environment settings
shift	Use extended batch file parameters
time	Set the time in the internal clock/calendar
type	Display the contents of a file

ver	Display the DOS version number
verify	Drive write verification toggle
vol	Display a drive volume label.

DOS commands are often followed by a drive or a file name or a path name. Some commands require a variety of these *arguments*, others require none. Also, some commands allow the use of optional *switches*, usually a slash and a letter to denote some additional action. The syntax, the way the commands must be typed, is described for each command according to the following conventions:

[d]	a drive specifier; usually **a:** (the memory card drive) or **c:** (the RAM drive). Includes a colon
[dir]	a directory on a drive
[fname]	a full file name and file extension separated by a dot
[path]	a combination of drive and directory. If no drive is included at the start of a path, the current drive is assumed. If no directory is included in the path, the current directory is assumed.
(/w)	parentheses are used to indicate an optional parameter which may be used with a particular command
. . .	ellipsis; indicates that more parameters may be included, following the pattern of those shown
[(/w)(/a)]	square brackets are used to indicate a range of options from which only one may be chosen.

APP

`app [(/a)(/c)(/d)(/e)(/s)(/w)]`

The **app** command is used to start the main application programs from DOS. You can either type:

```
app [Return]
```

to view the applications menu, or type app followed by a space, a slash (/) and the first character of the name of the application to be run:

`app /a [Return]`	Address Book
`app /c [Return]`	Calculator
`app /d [Return]`	Diary
`app /e [Return]`	Editor
`app /s [Return]`	Setup facility
`app /w [Return]`	Worksheet

The **app** command is most useful for auto-running an application from a batch file. For example, if the last line of the **autoexec.bat** file is:

```
app /w
```

then the worksheet is automatically started every time the **autoexec.bat** file is run.

BREAK

`break [(on)(off)]`

The **break** command allows DOS to check for the break key ([Fn] [B]) more frequently. The break key causes the Portfolio to stop its current activity.

The **break** command used on its own reports its current state, showing either:

```
BREAK is off
```

or:

```
BREAK is on
```

When the Portfolio is first used, break is off.

If you press the break key when break is off, the Portfolio will stop its current activity during input from the keyboard or output to the screen. If you press the break key when break is on, the Portfolio will also stop its current activity during certain drive operations.

CD (CHDIR) `cd [path]`

The **cd** command (you can also use the full form **chdir**) is used to change directory on the current drive.

The **cd** command may be used to change from any directory to any other directory, as long as the full pathname of the required directory is given. For example, if the root level directory contains the directories **\sales** and **\costs**, to change from **sales** to **costs**, type:

```
cd \costs [Return]
```

If you omit the backslash (\) DOS attempts to change to a directory called **costs** within the current directory.

To change from any directory or sub-directory to the root level directory, type:

```
cd \ [Return]
```

The **cd** command can also be used to change to the *parent directory*, the directory above the current directory, by typing:

```
cd.. [Return]
```

To determine the current drive and directory, just type cd [Return]. The current drive and directory are displayed on the screen.

CHKDSK `chkdsk [d]`

The **chkdsk** (check-disk) command is used to check the RAM drive or a memory card for errors. The **chkdsk** command should occasionally be used to check for errors on memory devices.

The **chkdsk** command also displays information regarding the number of files on the drive and the amount of free memory in the Portfolio. For example:

```
c>chkdsk
   62720 bytes total disk capacity
     256 bytes in 1 directories
    7680 bytes in 13 user files
   54784 bytes available on disk
  126976 bytes total memory
   47344 bytes free
c>
```

CLS

```
cls
```

The **cls** command is used to clear the Portfolio's screen. This command can be used at the DOS prompt or from within a batch file to clear the screen before printing some message.

COPY

```
copy [path][fname] [path][fname]
```

The **copy** command is used to copy one or more files from one location to another. The command is followed by two pathnames; the source and the destination. For example, to make a second copy of a file called **sales.txt** under the name **letter.txt**, you would type:

```
copy sales.txt letter.txt [Return]
```

To copy all of the files in the root level directory of **c:** to the memory card in **a:**, you would type:

```
copy c:\*.* a: [Return]
```

As the copy command is carried out by DOS, the names of the files being copied are displayed on the screen. At the end of the process, the number of files copied is shown.

DATE `date [mm/dd/yy]`

The Portfolio's internal clock/calendar keeps constant track of the date and time, even through leap years. However, should you need to change the date stored in the Portfolio, the **date** command allows you to do so.

Type **date** and press [Return]. The screen shows:

```
Date: Thu  8-09-1990
New date (mm/dd/yy):
```

You can now type the new date and press [Return]. Alternatively you can add the new date on the command line.

DEL `del [path][fname]`

The **del** (delete) command is used to delete files from a memory drive.

Note that when you have deleted a file, you cannot get it back! Once a file has been deleted, it has gone for good, so use this command with care.

For example, to delete from **c:** all of the files with the extension **.txt**, type:

```
del c:\*.txt [Return]
```

If no files are found which match your command, the screen shows the message **File not found**.

DIR

```
dir [path][fname] (/p)(/w)
```

The **dir** (directory) command lists the files and directories on a drive. The command lists the files on the default drive unless another drive and/or path is specified. For example, if the default drive is **c:**, type:

```
dir [Return]
```

to see the files on **c:**. The screen might show:

```
Volume in drive c is portfolio
Directory of c:\
system          <DIR>        8-09-90    10:00a
memo      txt        2458    8-09-90    10:30a
sales     wks       12534    8-09-90    10:40a
office    dry        6745    8-10-90    11:45a
letter1   txt        1812    8-10-90     4:40p
      5 Files 45283 bytes free
c>
```

The screen first shows the volume name of the default drive (see the **label** and **vol** commands later in this chapter). The screen then shows the path name for which the directory is to be listed and the list of files and directories.

Each item shows the name, the extension, the size in bytes and the date and time the file was created. The last line shows the number of files and the amount of free space on the drive.

If the drive has a large number of files, the list scrolls off the top of the screen too quickly for you to read the names and details. However, you can use the /p switch (paged) to see just one screen full, one page, at a time. For example, type:

```
dir /p [Return]
```

The screen shows:

```
Volume in drive c is portfolio
Directory of c:\
system        <DIR>       8-09-90   10:00a
memo     txt       2458   8-09-90   10:30a
sales    wks      12534   8-09-90   10:40a
Strike a key when ready ...
```

Press any key and the next page is shown:

```
office   dry       6745   8-10-90   11:45a
letter1  txt       1812   8-10-90    4:40p
      5 Files 45283 bytes free
```

Another way to see the list of files is in wide mode, using the /w switch. For example, type:

```
dir /w [Return]
```

The screen shows:

```
Volume in drive c is portfolio
Directory of c:\
system        memo     txt sales    wks
office   dry letter1  txt
      5 Files 45283 bytes free
c>
```

The files are shown in short form, with just the name and extension, in three columns across the screen. If there are still too many files to be seen in one screen-full, you can use the /p switch too, as described above.

You can use wild-cards to search for groups of files. For example:

`dir *.txt`	all files with the extension **.txt** on the default drive
`dir *.wk?`	all worksheet files, **.wks** and **.wk1**, on the default drive
`dir \txt\??.*`	all files with a name of two characters in the directory **\txt**.

See the description of the use of wild-cards earlier in this chapter.

ECHO

`echo [(on)(off)(text message)]`

The **echo** command is used to switch on or off the line-echo of commands in batch files, and to display a line of text on the screen from within a batch file. See also the section on batch files later in this chapter.

When a batch file is run, the commands in the file are displayed on the screen before they are carried out, just as if they had been typed at the keyboard; they are echoed to the screen. The default echo state is on. To switch the echo state off, include at the start of the file the command:

```
echo off
```

All subsequent commands are hidden and do not appear on the screen before they are executed.

The **echo** command can also be used to echo a line of text to the screen during execution of a batch file. For example, here is a batch file which prints a message on the screen and then deletes the Portfolio's clipboard and undelete files:

```
echo off
echo Deleting .dat files
del \system\undelete.dat
del \system\clipbord.dat
```

When the file is run, the message **Deleting .dat files** appears on the screen.

@ECHO

`@echo [(on)(off)(text message)]`

In the **echo** command described above, when the command is used initially to prevent all commands being echoed to the screen, the command itself still appears on screen. The **@echo** command works in the same way as the **echo** command, but the command itself is not echoed to the screen.

FDISK `fdisk [size]`

The **fdisk** command is used to rest the Portfolio's built-in RAM drive, **c:**. **When fdisk is used, all files on the RAM drive are lost, so use this command with caution!**.

You must specify a size for the RAM drive, as a number of kilobytes (1k is 1024 bytes). The minimum size is 8k and the maximum is the full amount of memory in the Portfolio minus a certain amount for system use. If you try to set the RAM drive to too large a size, the maximum size is displayed on the screen.

When you use the **fdisk** command, the screen displays a message advising you that all files will be lost and offering the chance to continue or cancel the command.

FOR/IN/DO `for %a in ([set]) do [comm.] %a`

The **for** command, used together with the **in** and **do** commands, provides a looping structure for use in batch files. In the syntax shown above, **%a** is a variable which is used in place of each of the files in **[set]**. The set of files may be ***.***, ***.txt** or any other valid DOS file specifier.

The **[comm.]** is any valid DOS command and the second occurrence of **%a** is the place where the individual file name will be associated with the given command.

See also the section on batch files later in this chapter.

FORMAT `format [d] (/v)`

The **format** command is used to prepare a memory card for use in the Portfolio. Before you try to store any information on a memory card, it must be **formatted** by using this command.

The formatting process organises the memory within the card and prepares it for the creation of DOS files and directories. All DOS memory devices can be given a volume name, the **/v** switch allows you to specify a volume name for the memory card when issuing the **format** command.

For example, to format the memory card in the drive, and give it the volume name **portfolio**, type:

```
format a: /v portfolio [Return]
```

See also the **vol** and **label** commands described later in this chapter.

GOTO `goto batchfilelabel`

The **goto** command is a branching structure for batch files. It can be used in conjunction with the **if** command described below.

When the **goto** command occurs in a batch file, execution jumps to the point in the file at which the given label appears. The label must appear elsewhere in the file, preceded by a colon. For example:

```
goto end
delete *.*
:end
```

No files would be deleted by this batch file because execution jumps straight from the first line to the label **:end**. Note that the label name used with the **goto** command does not have a colon, but the label itself starts with a colon.

IF

`if [condition] [command]`

The **if** command is a conditional structure command, primarily for use in batch files, although it can be used directly at the DOS prompt. It can be used in conjunction with the **goto** command to provide a conditional branch within a batch file.

The **if** command is used to check a condition and then, according to the result of that check, execute a command. The **if** command can be used in any of the following forms:

```
if [fname] exist [command]
if [fname] not exist [command]
if errorlevel [n] [command]
```

For example, this batch file checks that the file **letter1.txt** does not exist, before copying a form letter file to that name:

```
if not exist c:\sales\letter1.txt
copy \sales\formlet.txt letter1.txt
```

The form of the command using **errorlevel** checks the return value supplied by the previous external program. If the return value is greater than or equal to [n], the condition in the **if** command is **true**.

HELP

`help`

The **help** command is used to call up a list of all of the DOS commands according to type; file commands, directory commands and so on.

LABEL

`label [d] ([labelname])`

The **label** command is used to write a volume label to the RAM drive or a memory card. The label must be no more than 11 characters long and is automatically converted to lower case. Spaces are not allowed in volume labels.

For example, to write the volume label ttp-ltd to the RAM drive, **c:**, type:

```
label c: [Return]
ttp-ltd [Return]
```

To delete a volume label, just press [Return] when prompted for the volume label.

MD (MKDIR) `md [directory]`

The **md** command, or its full form **mkdir**, is used to make a new sub-directory in the current directory. For example, if the current directory is the root level directory on **c:**, to create a new directory called **marktg**, type:

```
md marktg [Return]
```

The directory is created and you can now create files in that directory, using the path \marktg.

OFF `off`

The **off** command, as the name suggests, switches the Portfolio off or, more properly, into standby mode.

When you switch on a desk-top computer, a program called **autoexec.bat** is automatically run. This does **not** happen when you switch on the Portfolio (by pressing any key). On the Portfolio, **autoexec.bat** is only run after a reset or when you explicitly run **autoexec**.

The **off** command is used purely to conserve battery power. However, note that the Portfolio automatically switches off if no keys have been pressed for more than two minutes and no other operation is being carried out.

The Portfolio may also be switched off by holding down the [Fn] key and pressing [O].

PAUSE `pause (text message)`

The **pause** command suspends execution of a batch file. When the command is encountered in a batch file, the screen shows the message **Strike a key when ready ....**

PATH `path [path](;[path])...`

The **path** command is used to set the path through which DOS searches for executable files. For example, your **autoexec.bat** file might contain the command:

```
path c:\;c:\utility
```

If you type:

```
dosedit [Return]
```

DOS searches for an executable file called dosedit in first the root level directory and then the directory called **utility**.

If there is more than one executable file with a given name, the following priority is used:

.com files
.exe files
.bat files.

To set the path so that only the default directory is searched for executable files, type:

```
path ; [Return]
```

PROMPT `prompt (prompttext)`

The prompt command is used to change the DOS prompt. When you first use the Portfolio, the prompt is just the current drive; **c:**. You can, however, change the prompt to any text string. You can also use a number of special characters as follows:

$$	the $ character
$b	the | character (bar)
$d	the date
$g	the > character (greater)
$h	backspace (BS)
$l	the < character (less)
$n	the current drive
$p	the current directory on the current drive
$s	the space character (leading only)
$t	the time
$v	the DOS version number
$_	a carriage return - line feed

If the **prompt** command is used without any following text, the default prompt is used.

RD (RMDIR) `rd [directory]`

The **rd** command, or its full form **rmdir**, is used to remove a directory from the directory tree structure on the current drive. To remove a directory, the directory must first be empty. Use the **del** command to delete files from a directory before using **rd**.

REM `rem (text remark)`

The **rem** command is used in batch files to insert a non-executable remark. For example:

```
rem deletes all .old files in \marktg
rem
del \marktg\*.old
```

REN `ren [oldfname] [newfname]`

The **ren** command is used to rename a file on a drive. For example, to rename the file **c:\marktg\quarter1.wks** as **c:\marktg\quarter1.old**, type:

```
ren c:\marktg\quarter1.wks
c:\marktg\quarter1.old [Return]
```

The screen shows:

```
C:\MARKTG\QUARTER1.WKS to
C:\MARKTG\QUARTER1.OLD
```

You can use the usual DOS wildcards to rename groups of files. For example, to rename all Worksheet files to have the extension **.old**, type:

```
ren *.wk? *.old [Return]
```

RUN `run [d][fname]`

The **run** command is not a normal DOS command, it is used on the Portfolio to run a program directly from a memory card. This command should only be used as directed by the user manual supplied with memory card software. The **run** command cannot be used to run **.exe** or **.com** programs.

SET `set [string1] = [string2]`

The **set** command is used to set certain system facilities. The **set** command on its own displays on the screen the current environment settings. For example, when the Portfolio is first used, if you type:

```
set [Return]
```

The screen shows:

```
PATH=
COMSPEC=\COMMAND.COM
```

This shows that no path has been set (see the **path** command earlier in this chapter) and that the current command interpreter is **command.com**. If you use the **prompt** command, described earlier in this chapter, the new prompt is also displayed by the **set** command.

The **set** command can also be used to make one string equivalent to another.

SHIFT `shift`

The **shift** command is used it batch files to make ten further parameters available from the command line, in addition to the usual ten.

When a batch file is run, you can add a parameter, the value of which is passed into the batch file itself. For example, you could create a batch file, with the name **d.bat**, which deletes a file specified by a command line parameter. If your batch file **d.bat** contains:

```
del %1
```

To delete a file called **letter.old**, you would type:

```
d letter.old [Return]
```

The parameter, **letter.old**, is passed from the command line into the batch file.

The following batch file, **backup.bat**, backs up all files in a number of directories on **c:** to directories with the same names on **a:**:

```
copy %1\*.* a:%1
copy %2\*.* a:%1
copy %3\*.* a:%1
...
copy %9\*.* a:%1
```

So to back up all files in the directories **\lett**, **\sheets**, **\marktg**,... and **\system**, ten directories in all, you would type:

```
backup \lett \sheets \marktg...  \system
[Return]
```

However, you might need to back up more than 9 directories, so the following batch file, using **shift**, allows for a further ten parameters:

```
copy %1\*.* a:%1
copy %2\*.* a:%1
copy %3\*.* a:%1
 ...
copy %9\*.* a:%1
shift
shift
 ...
shift
shift        (ten shifts in all)
copy %0\*.* a:%1
copy %1\*.* a:%1
copy %2\*.* a:%1
copy %3\*.* a:%1
 ...
copy %9\*.* a:%1
```

Note that the original parameter called %0 is used to pass the name of the batch file (without the **.bat** extension).

TIME `time (hh:mm:ss:xx)`

The **time** command is used to set the time stored by the Portfolio's internal clock/calendar.

Type the command alone and the screen shows:

```
Time: 10:30:25.00
New time:
```

You can now type the time in the format hh:mm:ss:xx, where xx represents hundredths of seconds. You can omit the latter parts of the time, so for exactly 10am, you would type:

```
10 [Return]
```

For 4:35pm you would type:

```
16:35 [Return]
```

and so on.

TYPE `type [fname] (/p)`

The **type** command is used to display the whole contents of a file on the screen.

If the file is too long to fit on the screen in one go, the text scrolls off the top of the screen too quickly for you to read. However, you can use the /p switch (paged) to see just one screen full, one page, at a time. For example, type:

```
type \marktg\report.txt /p [Return]
```

The screen shows the first few lines of the file and then the message **Strike a key when ready ....**

VER `ver`

The **ver** command displays the DOS version number on the screen:

```
DIP Operating System x.xx  vx.xxx
Copyright (c) DIP 1989
```

VERIFY `verify [(off)(on)]`

The **verify** command is used to determine or set the disk-write verify state. When verify is on, all data written to a disk (memory device) is verified at the time of writing.

You can either type verify and press [Return] to determine the verify state, or set the state with verify on, or off. The default state is verify off.

VOL `vol [d]`

The **vol** command reads the volume name from a drive and displays it on the screen. If **vol** is used without a drive designator, the volume name of the default drive is read.

BATCH FILES

A batch file is a collection of DOS commands in a plain-text ASCII file. All batch files have the file extension **.bat**. The batch file can be executed from the DOS prompt, causing all of the commands in the file to be passed to DOS one by one.

Any of the DOS commands described in this chapter can be used in batch files, but the following DOS commands are most useful within batch files:

echo	**for**	**goto**
if	**pause**	**rem**
shift		

How Batch Files Work

When you type a DOS command at the DOS prompt, it is carried out immediately by the command interpreter. Even if the command is long and complex, it must be completely correct or it will not work, or, worse than that, it might do the wrong thing.

One way around the problem of typing long and complicated DOS commands, especially those used frequently, is to put the commands into batch files.

You can create a batch file in two ways; by using the **copy** command or by using the Portfolio's Editor.

Copying to a Batch File

You might want to create a batch file called **go.bat** which deletes any files with the extension **.old**, copies your diary file to a backup memory card and starts the Worksheet. To copy those commands from the keyboard into a batch file, type:

```
copy con go.bat [Return]
```

and then type the commands themselves:

```
del \marktg\*.old [Return]
del \sheets\*.old [Return]
copy \system\diary.dry a: [Return]
app /w [Ctrl][Z] [Return]
```

The last line is ended by a Control Z (hold down [Ctrl] and press [Z]) and then a press of [Return]; all the other lines are ended by a press of [Return].

The problem with making a batch file in this way is that the commands must be exactly right, because you cannot go back and alter a line after you have pressed [Return].

Batch Files in The Editor

The other way to create a batch file is to use the Portfolio's built-in text editor. Start the Editor in the usual way and start a clean, new document with the **Files: New** command.

Type in the same list of commands shown above, pressing [Return] at the end of each line, except the last. You do not have to use the [Ctrl][Z] used above to end the file.

Use the **Files: Save as** command to save the file with the name **go.bat** - remember to specify the extension **.bat** or the Editor will use **.txt**. Now when you exit from the Editor, you can use the command **go**, just like a DOS command.

Batch File Parameters

One useful feature of batch files is the ability to pass the name of a file from DOS into the batch file. For example, the **rd** command (remove directory) does not let you remove a directory unless that directory is empty; you could create a batch file which deletes all files in any directory and then removes the directory.

Use the Editor, as described above, to create this batch file:

```
if exist %1\*.* del %1\*.*
rd %1
```

Save the file under the name **dd.bat** (delete directory). Now when you want to delete all the files in a directory and remove the directory all in one go, just type dd followed by the name of the directory, for example:

```
dd oldfiles [Return]
```

If there are any files in the given directory, the batch file deletes them, asking you to confirm the deletion. However, see also the section below on INPUT REDIRECTION for how to prevent this confirmation check.

OUTPUT REDIRECTION

There are a large number of DOS commands which result in some form of output; **dir**, **type**, **chkdsk** and so on. All of these commands can have that output directed, not to the screen, but to a file or another DOS device, such as a printer or a file.

This redirection of output is carried out by using the > character. For example, to redirect output from the **dir** command to the printer, you would type:

```
dir > prn [Return]
```

Where **prn** is the DOS device name for the printer. See the section on device names earlier in this chapter.

To direct the output from **dir** to a file, you could type:

```
dir > filename.ext [Return]
```

Where **filename.ext** is the file to which the output will be directed. If no file exists by that name, a new one is automatically created. **If there is already a file with that name, that file will be overwritten with the output from the command.**

Rather than overwriting an existing file, you can specify that the output is to be **appended** to the file, by typing:

```
dir >> filename.ext [Return]
```

If a file with the given name does not exist, a new one is created, otherwise the output is added to the end of the file.

INPUT REDIRECTION

DOS allows you to redirect the output from a DOS command to some destination other than the screen. You can also redirect input **from** a source other than the keyboard. For example, in the description of batch files above, this file appeared:

```
if exist %1\*.* del %1\*.*
rd %1
```

This batch file checks for the existence of files in a given directory, deletes the files and then removes the directory. However, the DOS **del** command used in the first line, demands confirmation when using the form **del *.*** (ie all files). To get around this confirmation check, change the file to read:

```
if exist %1\*.* del %1\*.* < yes.txt
rd %1
```

Now create another file called **yes.txt**. Into the file type:

```
y [Return]
```

It is important that you press return after the single text character in the file.

Now when you run the new version of the batch file above, the files in the given directory are deleted immediately. The confirmation check still occurs, but the y (yes) which confirms the deletion comes from the file **yes.txt**.

5

THE ADDRESS BOOK

THE BASICS

The Portfolio's Address Book stores names, addresses and telephone numbers in alphabetical order. The only limit on the size of an Address Book file, and on the number of Address Book files you keep, is the amount of free memory in your Portfolio.

You can search an Address Book file for any name or address, or even part of a telephone number. You can select just a sub-set of the entries in the current Address Book file, perhaps all of the overseas numbers, and then save them as another Address Book file.

The Address Book will even dial telephone numbers for you, on any tone-dial telephone system, with its built-in tone dialler. All you have to do is find the entry in the file, hold the handset against the speaker and make a single keypress.

THE FIRST SCREEN

When you start the Address Book for the first time the screen shows:

```
C:UNNAMED.ADR                                    #0




Thu 09 Aug 90 10:30
```

As always in the applications, the top line of the frame shows the current file name, **unnamed.adr**, and the number of **records** in the current Address Book file. Again, just like in the other applications, press [F5] (hold down [Fn] and press 5) to remove the screen frame.

Of course, because you have just started the Address Book for the first time, the file **unnamed.adr** is empty, so the cursor is at the top of the screen and the number of records shows 0.

The Address Book automatically gives files the extension **.adr** (see chapters 2 and 4 for more details of files and file extensions).

TYPING A NEW RECORD

To type a new record into the Address Book, first press [Tab] to start a blank record. The screen shows:

```
C:UNNAMED.ADR                                    #0
______________________________________________________



Thu 09 Aug 90 10:30
```

Now type a name with a telephone number and address. For example:

```
HM The Queen (0753) 99998 [Return]
Windsor Castle [Return]
WINDSOR [Return]
Berkshire [Return]
England [Return]
```

The screen now shows:

```
C:UNNAMED.ADR ══════════════════ #1 ≈
HM The Queen (0753) 99998
──────────────────────────────────────
Windsor Castle
WINDSOR
Berkshire
England
Thu 09 Aug 90 10:30 ══════════════════
```

The top line shows the name and number of your friend. **Whenever you type in a name and number, you must separate the name and number with a space**. The local dialling code is included in brackets, followed by the telephone number. Subsequent lines hold your friend's address.

Screen Mode

At the moment, the screen shows one whole address. This is called **Screen** mode. One record is shown in full. If you type in a very long record, just keep pressing [Return] at the end of each line, the address will scroll up as you go. There is no limit to the number of lines in one record. Press [Esc] at any time to change to Line mode.

Line Mode

Press [Esc] and the display changes to **Line** mode. This shows just the name and number on one line, leaving the rest of the screen to display other names and numbers. At the moment, you have only one record in your file, so just HM The Queen appears on the screen. As you add records, these are automatically shown on the screen in alphabetical order. Press [Return] on any record to change to Screen mode for that record.

ADDING MORE RECORDS

At this stage, you might like to add a few more names and addresses to the file. If the display is in Screen mode, press [Esc] to change to Line mode. To start a new record, press [Tab]. The screen clears and you are in a new blank record, ready to type a name, number and address.

At the end of a new record, press [Esc] to return to Line mode or press [Pg Dn] (hold down [Fn] and press [↓]) to add another record.

It doesn't matter where in the file the cursor is positioned when you add a record, and it doesn't matter in what order you add the records - the Address Book automatically sorts them into alphabetical order. Records which start with a number, for example, 4-Square Building Co, appear after the alphabetically sorted records. Last are any records starting with any character other than a letter or a digit.

EDITING A RECORD

When you have entered a record, you might want to change some of the details. For example, in the record above for HM The Queen, you might want to add an alternative number at the end of the top line.

If the display is not in Screen mode, press [Return]. The screen again shows:

```
C:UNNAMED.ADR ════════════════════ #1 ≈
HM The Queen (0753) 99998
─────────────────────────────────────────
Windsor Castle
WINDSOR
Berkshire
England
Thu 09 Aug 90 10:30 ═══════════════════
```

To change any line, just use the cursor keys to move to that line and type away. You can move to any line and edit any line in a record. You can also add new lines to the end of a record, but you cannot delete a line from the middle of a record or add new lines in the middle of a record.

In our example, move to the end of the top line and type:

```
/9
```

Press [Esc] to return to Line mode.

You can also use the following keyboard shortcuts to delete various portions of text:

Key Press	**Action**
[Ctrl] [B]	Delete back to start of line
[Ctrl] [E]	Delete to end of line
[Ctrl] [L]	Delete whole of current line
[Ctrl] [W]	Delete word to right of cursor
[Ctrl] [BS]	Delete word to left of cursor

DELETING A RECORD

If you find that a record is no longer required, you can delete it with a single keypress. With the display in Line mode, move the cursor to the record to be deleted and press [Del/Ins]. The record is immediately deleted and the following records moved up to close the gap.

Don't worry if you accidentally delete the wrong record, just press [F4] to undelete the record. When you undelete a record in this way, the display changes to Screen mode and the record appears on the screen as if it had been retyped at the keyboard.

MOVING AROUND

There are a number of key-presses which enable you to move around an Address Book file quickly and easily. When the display is in Screen mode, you can move to the next record by pressing [Pg Dn], or the previous record by typing [Pg Up].

When the display is in Line mode, the following moves are available:

Key Press	Action
[Ctrl] [A]	Go to start of current file
[Ctrl] [U]	Return to previous cursor position
[Ctrl] [Z]	Go to end of current file
[Fn] [↑]	Move up one screen
[Fn] [↓]	Move down one screen

You can also move to the first record starting with any letter by pressing that letter. For example, to move to the first entry starting with S, perhaps San Silvestre, just press [S]. Press [S] again and the cursor moves on to the next record starting with S.

Taking this one step further, press [Z] to move the cursor to the first record starting with the letter Z. However, as there may not be any records starting with Z, you can use [Z] to go to the last record in the file.

THE FUNCTION KEYS

The function keys [F1] to [F5] have the usual uses in the Address Book:

[F1]	Display the Address Book command menu
[F2]	Request Help
[F3]	View the clipboard menu
[F4]	Undelete the last item deleted
[F5]	Zoom the screen frame on or off.

The function keys [F6] to [F10] are not used in the Address Book.

SEARCHING THE ADDRESS BOOK

When you have entered all of your names and addresses, you will need to be able to find a particular record as quickly as possible. In the previous section, a number of keyboard shortcuts are listed. These let you move rapidly around a file, but do not let you search the file.

The **Search** command in the Address Book main command menu allows you to search the current file for any piece of text, whether it is in the first line of a record or deep down in the address. You can even search for part of a telephone number.

The **Search** command is described later in this chapter.

AUTO-DIALLING

The Address Book has a built-in auto-dialler which will operate any tone-dial (DTMF) telephone. Any Address Book record which has a telephone number on the first line can be auto-dialled.

In the example we used earlier in this chapter, the first line, containing the name and telephone number, was:

```
HM The Queen (0753) 99998/9
```

The telephone number appears in the usual format with the local dialling code in brackets followed by the specific telephone number.

When the display is in Line mode, move the cursor to the record you want to auto-dial and press [Ctrl] [D]. The screen shows, for example:

```
HM The Queen
(0753)99998
99998
(0753)99999
99999
Edit
```

The window shows the dialling code followed by the telephone number, the telephone number on its own, the dialling code with the alternative number and the alternative number on its own. This means that whether you are in the area of the Castle or otherwise, you can dial either number very easily.

Just move the cursor to the version you want to dial, hold the mouthpiece of the telephone next to the Portfolio's speaker (beside the screen) and press [Return].

If you know that The Queen is visiting the Royal Art Collection today and that the number of the Art Gallery at the Castle is 99997, select Edit from the window (press [E]) to edit any of the numbers shown.

Spaces in telephone numbers are treated by the Address Book as pauses in the number. International numbers do benefit from the insertion of occasional pauses, so just insert a space between groups of digits when you type in the number.

Note that the built-in auto-dialler works only on tone-dial telephone systems.

TELEPHONE NUMBER FORMATS

Above we saw how to auto-dial an telephone number stored in the Address Book, but so far we have not looked at the format in which the numbers must be stored.

Basically you can use the format we used earlier; the local dialling code in brackets followed by the telephone number. As we saw, the auto-dialler interprets this correctly and offers both formats for dialling - with and without the local dialling code. There are, however, a number of other ways in which you can organise your telephone numbers.

Alternative Numbers

Some numbers might have more than one incoming line, allowing you to dial 99995, 99996, 99997, 99998 and 99999. You don't want to clutter up your Address Book with such long strings of numbers, so you can use a slash to denote an alternative number. In this example, instead of:

```
HM The Queen (0753) 99995, 99996, 99997,
99998, 99999
```

you could enter:

```
HM The Queen (0753) 99995/6/7/8/9
```

The auto-dialler counts back from the end of the number, the required digits to make up the complete list. The example above would give the following options in the auto-dialler window:

```
(0753)99995
99995
(0753)99996
99996
(0753)99997
99997
(0753)99998
99998
(0753)99999
99999
Edit
```

You could even use a single local dialling code followed by different telephone numbers which are separated by a slash. For example, the dialling code for Windsor is 0753, so you could enter:

```
HM The Queen (0753) 99997/11111
```

The auto-dialler window would show the options:

```
(0753)99997
99997
(0753)11111
11111
Edit
```

Adding Text

The first line of the record contains the name and telephone number, but how do you distinguish between different telephone numbers where there are a number of options? The answer is to add text enclosed in square brackets. For example, you might have a general number for the Castle and a direct number for HRH's private facsimile machine. You could enter:

```
HM The Queen (0753) 99999, 99991 [fax]
```

The auto-dialler window would show the options:

```
(0753)99999
99999
(0753)99991 [fax]
99991 [fax]
Edit
```

You might want to put some additional text into the first line of the record, but which doesn't appear in the auto-dialler window. Put this text in square brackets **before** the dialling code and number. For example, if your entry read:

```
HM The Queen (0753) 99999, [fax] 99991
```

The auto-dialler window would show the options:

```
(0753)99999
99999
(0753)99991
99991
Edit
```

So the text appears when the record is displayed in Line or Screen mode, but does not appear in the auto-dial window.

Note: If, when you use the auto-dialler, the dialling code or the telephone number appears on the top line of the window frame as part of the name, you have omitted the space between the name and number. If there is no other number in the first line, the auto-dialler window is shown blank.

If you regularly use a telephone which requires a prefix on all numbers, perhaps an in-house exchange which requires you to dial 9 for an outside line, you can set a global prefix of up to 9 digits using the **Cards: Dial Prefix** command. See the description of the **Dial Prefix** command later in this chapter.

SELECTING RECORDS

You can keep as many Address Book files as you wish, subject only to the amount of free memory in your Portfolio. You might want to keep a separate file for home and business contacts, or you might have a separate file for overseas contacts.

You can also choose to keep all of your contacts in one file, just tagging each one with some special character or characters. For example, you could put into each record the characters *O for Overseas, *H for Home and *B for Business contacts.

You might open the file and just want to look at the overseas contacts. You can select all of the records containing the characters *O. The file then appears to contain only those selected records. You can then, if you wish, write the selected records to a new, separate file. Alternatively, you can return to the original file, cancelling the selection.

Selecting records is described later in this chapter under the heading The Cards: Select Command.

THE ADDRESS BOOK COMMANDS

This section describes each of the Address Book commands. To see the Address Book command menu, press [F1]. The screen shows:

```
                              Gen M:1 #0

                                       0
 Thu 09 Aug 90 10:30  NUM ====== INS
```

THE FILES MENU

When you select **Files** from the Address Book command menu, the screen shows:

```
Files
New
Load...
Save as...
Merge...
Write Selected
Print
```

The use of the **Files** commands is very much the same in each of the file-based applications. A full description of using these commands can be found in chapter 3 under the heading THE FILES COMMANDS. This section gives a brief round-up of the description found there.

The Files: New Command

If you have made any changes to the current file since it was last saved, the file changed symbol will be shown at the upper right corner of the screen frame. If you then select the **Files: New** command, the Portfolio prompts you to save the file, complete with its changes. The screen shows:

```
Save Current?
Yes
No
```

Select **Yes** to save the file under the current file name (shown on the top line of the screen frame), or select **No** to discard the current file **including any changes you have made since the last time the file was saved**.

The Files: Load Command

The **Files: Load** command is used to load an existing file from a drive into an application. A copy of the file is made from the original which is stored on the drive - loading a file does not have any effect on the original file, unlike saving (see the **Files: Save as** command below).

When you select the **Files: Load** command, the Portfolio prompts you to enter the name of the file you want to load. The screen shows:

```
═══════════ Load ═══════════
Name: C:\CONTAC\UNNAMED.ADR
```

The default file name (shown in the dialogue box) is always the file name most recently used by the current application program. If the current file name is, for example, **unnamed.adr**, that is the file name offered by the dialogue box. You now have four options:

1. Press [Return] to load the file shown in the dialogue box

2. Edit the file name to that of the file you want to load

3. Press the [*] key to see all files from the current application

4. Press the [:] key to see a list of all of the files and sub-directories found in the current directory.

Note that item 3 in the list above is the equivalent to typing *.* (see chapter 4 for more details of this in relation to DOS). You can also type a new, full path name with or without a file name, including wildcards, just like those used in DOS.

The Files: Save as Command

The **Files: Save as** command is used to save a copy of the current file under the same or a different name on any drive. If there is already a copy of the file under the name you use, **the old copy will be overwritten by the new copy**, so make sure you are not losing some vital information by using an existing file name.

If you save a new copy of a file under a name different from that of the original file, then the original file will be unaffected when you make your new copy.

For further details of the way in which file names are given, refer to the section above under the heading The Files: Load Command.

Note: The Golden Rule when using any type of computer is this - and there are no exceptions:

- **Always make a back-up copy of any file which is really important.**

You can make a copy onto a memory card or via the optional communications link to a desk-top pc. Then if disaster strikes, you still have a copy of your data.

The Files: Merge Command

Sometime it is useful to merge one file with another, to make a single larger file. The new file can then be saved to a drive as a new single file. To merge two files you use the **Files: Merge** command.

When you use the **Merge** command, the selected file is combined with the current file and the new file is then alphabetically sorted. When you select **Merge** from the **Files** menu, the screen shows:

```
Merge
Name:
```

You now have three options:

1. Press the [*] key to see all files from the current application

2. Press the [:] key to see a list of all of the files and sub-directories found in the current directory

3. Type the name of the document you want to merge with the current file.

Note that item 1 in the list above is the equivalent to typing *.* (see chapter 4 for more details of this in relation to DOS). You can also type a new, full path name with or without a file name, including wildcards, just like those used in DOS.

When you have selected a file, the file is combined with the current file and you can continue using and editing the resulting file. The current file name is not changed during this operation, and the original copies of the first file and the merged file are unaffected.

The Files: Write Selected Command

You can keep as many Address Book files as you wish, subject only to the amount of free memory in your Portfolio. You might want to keep a separate file for home and business contacts, or you might have a separate file for overseas contacts.

You can also choose to keep all of your contacts in one file, just tagging each one with some special character or characters. For example, you could put into each record the characters *O for Overseas, *H for Home and *B for Business contacts.

To select a sub-set of the records in the current file, use the **Cards: Select** command described later in this chapter. Having made a selection, you have two options:

1. Use the selected records for one session and abandon the selection when you leave the Address Book

2. Write the selected records as a new file on a drive, leaving the original, larger file intact.

If you decide to leave the Address Book, and do not want to keep the selected records as a separate file, just press [Esc] when the display is in Line mode. The selection is cancelled and the full, original file is now available again (in Line mode). Press [Esc] the leave the Address Book.

If you decide that the selection of records deserves to be stored as a separate file in its own right, select the **Write Selected** command from the **Files** menu. The screen shows:

```
Write
File:
```

You can now type a file name to be used for this selection of records. See the description of the **Files: Load** command above and in chapter 3 for full details of specifying file names. **Remember to use a different file name to the one used for the original file!**

When the new file is safely saved on a drive. You can press [Esc] to cancel the current selection in the original file, then use the **Files: Load** command to load the selection file.

The Files: Print Command

The **Print** command is used to print the contents of the current file to a printer (serial or parallel) or to a file on a drive. For more information on the destination of your printed output, see the section under the heading PREPARING TO PRINT in chapter 9.

When the **Print** command is selected, the whole of the current file is printed. However, if you have made a selection from the current file, just the selected records are printed.

Note that the margins and page length of the printed output are taken from the current settings made in the Portfolio's Setup facility. See chapter 9 for further details of Setup.

Printing With Postscript

Many offices now use laser printers instead of the old daisy-wheel or dot-matrix printers. Laser printers are quieter than impact printers and often a great deal faster. The print quality is very high and a great number of print styles are available. Some of the most impressive of these printers use the page description language PostScript.

The Portfolio's Address Book is not equipped to drive these laser printers to the limit but, with a little effort, the Portfolio can use them to very good effect. In chapter 13 you will find details of a disk containing a suite of PostScript programs which enable you to print Address Book files, business graphs and a variety of special type styles from the Portfolio.

THE SEARCH COMMAND

When you have a large Address Book file, it is usually possible to go straight to the record you want. Just press the first letter of the name. For the record for David & Julia, just press [D]; the cursor moves directly to the first record starting with D. You can then step down through the D's, using the [↓] key.

The problems begin when you want to find the telephone number of the Veterinary surgeon, but his number is alongside his business name - and you can't remember the name... Perhaps the record reads:

```
Starcate Associates (0757) 959207
Malcolm Maclean, Veterinary Surgeon
```

The business name is on the first line with the telephone number, but you can only recall that you want to speak to Malcolm. The **Search** command allows you to search for any text or number, anywhere in a record. This means that you can find a record however little of the detail you can remember.

When you select **Search** from the Address Book menu, the screen shows:

```
═══════ Search ═══════
For:
```

You can now type the part of the record you can remember, called a **search string**, followed by [Return]. It doesn't matter if you use upper or lower case letters, the Address Book ignores case when searching. So in the example above, you could type MALCOLM, malc, Vet, VETERINARY, Mac, or any other part of the record. If you happened to remember the dialling code, you could even type that - 0757.

When you press [Return], the cursor moves to the first record containing the text you typed.

There are two things to be aware of when searching:

- If you type a long search string, the chances of a typing error are greater. You might also type MALCOLM when the record only contains the name MALC - so the search will fail

- If you type a short search string, the chances of the wrong record being found are increased. For example, typing MA as your search string would find the record you want, but it would also find records containing Mary, Maggie, Mark, Bank Manager and so on.

There is obviously a happy medium which gives you the greatest chance of finding the record you want. Try to use the most unique piece of text in the record, perhaps VETER or SURGEON.

The example above is just concerned with finding a single record, but you might want to find several records using the same search string. For example, you might want to ring around the family to organise a get-together. If all of your records of the family contain, as the last line, the text, *F, you can just search for that text.

The cursor moves the the first record containing *F. You call the number of Uncle Jim, then press [Ctrl] [S]. This repeats the most recent search and finds the next occurrence of the same text. The cursor moves to the record for Aunt Nancy, you call her and then press [Ctrl] [S] again - the cursor moves on to Cousin Angela and so on.

You can code all of your records this way, using some unique piece of text. A star is used here as an example, you could use any text you wish, as long as it is unlikely to naturally occur in the middle of some other record.

If you press [Ctrl] [S] when you haven't already used the **Search** command, the search window is presented and you can type a search string.

See also the description of the **Cards: Select** command later in this chapter.

THE CARDS MENU

The **Cards** menu contains commands which let you insert a new record (or card), erase a record, select a number of records according to their content and enter a dial-prefix which is used before all auto-dialled numbers.

When you select **Cards** from the Address Book command menu, the screen shows:

```
═══ Cards ═══
Insert
Erase
Select
Dial Prefix... 9
```

The Cards: Insert Command

The **Insert** command has the same effect as pressing the [Tab] key when the display is in Line mode; the screen clears to show a new, empty record, into which you can type a name, number and address.

It doesn't matter where the cursor is in the file, the new record will automatically be placed into its correct alphabetical position in the file.

When you have typed your new record, press [Esc] to return to Line mode, or press [Pg Dn] to add the record to the file and start another new record.

The Cards: Erase Command

The **Erase** command has the same effect as pressing the [Del/Ins] key when the display is in Line mode; the current record is erased from the file.

To erase any single record from the file, first move the cursor to the record you want to erase, in Line or Screen mode, and select **Erase** from the **Cards** menu. The record is immediately erased; in Line mode, the cursor moves on to the next record; in Screen mode, the next record is displayed in full.

The Cards: Select Command

If you keep all of your contacts in one file, you might like to tag each record with some special character or characters.

For example, you could put into each record the characters *O for Overseas, *H for Home and *B for Business contacts.

You might open the file and just want to look at the overseas contacts. You can use the **Select** command to select all of the records containing the characters *O. The file then appears to contain only those selected records.

When you choose the **Select** command from the **Cards** menu, the screen shows:

```
═══════════ Select ═══════════
All:
```

You can now type a piece of text which will be the basis of the selection. For example, if you type (01) and press [Return], the Address Book will select from the current file just the records which contain the text (01). The current file then appears to contain just the selected records, but at the top right of the screen frame, the number of selected records and the number of records in the whole file are shown as, for example, **#27 of 315**.

To abandon the selection and return to the full file, press [Esc] when the display is in Line mode. The number of records returns to normal and the whole file is again available.

See also the **Files: Write Selected** command described earlier in this chapter.

The Cards: Dial Prefix Command

If you have to dial numbers from an in-house exchange, you may have to dial 9 or some other digit for the exchange to assign you an outside line. The **Dial Prefix** command allows you to specify one or more digits as a dial prefix (up to 9 digits). The dial prefix is then automatically dialled before any auto-dialled numbers. If you then move to a telephone or an exchange which does not require this prefix, you must select the command again and delete the prefix.

When you select the **Dial Prefix** command from the **Cards** menu, the screen shows:

```
╔═══ Dial prefix ═══╗
║ 9 Figures max:    ║
╚═══════════════════╝
```

You can now enter a dial prefix of up to 9 digits and spaces. The spaces indicate a pause; one or two can be useful after the prefix, to allow the exchange time to allocate you a line.

When a dial prefix has been set, it appears at the top right of the screen frame next to the number of records in the file.

THE DIAL COMMAND

The Address Book has a built-in auto-dialler which will operate any tone-dial (DTMF) telephone. Any Address Book record which has a telephone number on the first line can be auto-dialled.

When the display is in Line mode, move the cursor to the record you want to auto-dial and select **Dial** from the Address Book command menu (or just press [Ctrl] [D]). The screen shows, for example:

```
HM The Queen
(0753)99998
99998
(0753)99999
99999
Edit
```

The window shows the dialling code followed by the telephone number, the telephone number on its own, the dialling code with the alternative number and the alternative number on its own.

Just move the cursor to the version you want to dial, hold the mouthpiece of the telephone next to the Portfolio's speaker (beside the screen) and press [Return].

If you know that The Queen is visiting the Royal Art Collection today and that the number of the Art Gallery at the Castle is 99997, select Edit from the window (press [E]) to edit any of the numbers shown.

Note that the built-in auto-dialler works only on tone-dial telephone systems.

For full details of the telephone number formats you can use, see the section earlier in this chapter under the heading TELEPHONE NUMBER FORMATS.

THE HELP COMMAND

The Portfolio has two built-in help systems. The first is accessible when using the application programs - just press [F2] (hold down [Fn] and press [2]). This system gives help on the keyboard, clipboard, undeleting and the function keys.

The second help system is available from the main command menu in each of the application programs, where the last command is **Help**.

When you select Help from the Address Book command menu, the screen shows:

```
Help
Address Book Menu
File handling
Dialing
```

The first menu option gives help on the Address Book command menu and its sub-menus. The second option gives specific help on the use of the **Files** commands, concerned with loading and saving files. The last option gives help on the Address Book's auto-dialling facility.

In each of the three help options, the help is in the form of a text file which you can read through by pressing the [↑] and [↓] keys. To return from one of the help files to the Help menu, press [Esc].

6

THE CALCULATOR

The Portfolio has a powerful built-in calculator with an editable 'tape'. The Calculator has all of the usual arithmetic operators (+, -, /, *), plus five memories, brackets, square roots, percentage breakdowns, one-key negation, factorials and optional printer output.

All output from the Calculator can be sent to a printer via an optional communications adapter, or printed to a file.

THE FIRST SCREEN

When you start the Calculator for the first time the screen shows:

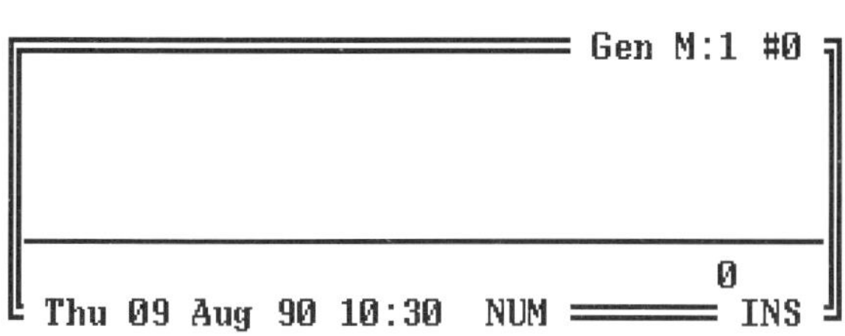

The top line of the frame shows the current numeric format, the number of the current memory and the number of elements in the current calculation. More about these later. Just like in the other applications, you can press [F5] (hold down [Fn] and press 5) to remove the screen frame, (press [F5) again to return the frame to view).

The upper part of the screen is used to display the numbers and operators. The lower part of the screen is the *result window*.

THE NUMERIC KEYPAD

The Portfolio's keyboard has the digits 0 to 9 arranged along the top row. This is the same as an ordinary typewriter keyboard. However, when using a calculator, it is easier to use a keypad where all of the digits and arithmetic signs are gathered together. The Portfolio has just such a keypad, with the legends printed in magenta at the right of the keyboard.

In the other applications and in DOS, to use the numeric keypad, along with the arithmetic signs, hold down the [Fn] key and press the [N] key; this puts the keyboard into Numeric mode.

When you use the Portfolio Calculator, the keyboard is automatically set in Numeric mode and automatically returns to Normal mode when you leave the Calculator. So on the screen shown above, the keyboard status indicators on the bottom line of the screen frame show that the keyboard is in Numeric mode and Insert mode.

SIMPLE CALCULATIONS

The basic arithmetic operators which you can use are as follows:

+	plus
–	minus
*	multiply
/	divide

Let's go straight in and do a few calculations. When the Calculator screen is shown as above, type:

```
1+2+3 [Return]
```

The screen shows:

```
═══════════════════════════ Gen M:1 #3
                                 1  +
                                 2  +
                                 3
───────────────────────────────────────
                                 6  =
 Thu 09 Aug 90 10:30  NUM ═════ INS
```

You only press [Return] at the end of the calculation, to produce a final result - not after each number. An interim result is displayed in the result window as you type each stage of the calculation. Note also that the number of steps in the current calculation, 3, is displayed on the top line of the screen frame.

If at any stage you type a wrong number, just press [Esc] to clear the number, then type the correct number.

Now press [Esc] to clear the current calculation and type:

```
1+2*1+2 [Return]
```

When you press [Return], the result 5 is displayed in the result window. But what if you had intended to calculate 1+2 *times* 1+2, giving a result of 9? You would then need to type:

```
(1+2)*(1+2) [Return]
```

This shows that the calculation inside the brackets should be performed *before* the calculation outside the brackets;

The first 1+2 is calculated, then the second 1+2 and finally the two results are multiplied, giving the result 9.

This time the screen shows:

```
                                   Gen M:1 #4
                                       ( 1  +
                                         2 )*
                                       ( 1  +
                                         2 )
 ---------------------------------------------
                                         9
 Thu 09 Aug 90 10:30   NUM               INS
```

You can use up to about 20 sets of brackets in a single calculation, depending on the operators used within the brackets. If you use too many sets, a **Stack Full** error is displayed on the screen; press [Esc] to remove the error message and try making your calculation less complex.

EDITING THE TAPE

As you type in a calculation made up of a large number of steps, the interim steps, both numbers and operators, are displayed in the upper part of the screen.

As the steps in the calculation scroll off the top of the upper part of the screen, they are all stored in memory. You could think of them as being stored on a tape which scrolls off the screen and into the Portfolio's memory. When you have finished your calculation, or even between one step and the next, you can go back and look at or change the previous steps recorded on the tape.

At any time during a calculation, press the [↑] key to move the cursor into the upper part of the screen. You can now move the cursor around to any of the previous steps in the current calculation. You can just look at the previous steps and then return to the result window, or you can edit the previous steps.

If you choose to edit the previous steps, you can change the numbers or the arithmetic operators or both. You can even add new sets of brackets or delete existing ones (but make sure any left bracket has a corresponding right bracket).

To delete one whole line of the calculation (a number, with or without a bracket, and an operator) press [Ctrl] [L].

If you have changed one of the steps in your calculation and then decide to change it back to its original form, press the [Esc] key. The line is restored. However, note that if you change a line and then move on to another line, you cannot restore the previous line by pressing [Esc].

If, after editing the tape, you want to continue adding to the current calculation, add an operator as the last step in the calculation.

When you have edited the tape, if the cursor is still positioned somewhere on the tape, press [Return] to return the cursor to the result window. Any changes you have made to the steps of your calculation will then be reflected in the new result displayed.

THE FUNCTION KEYS

In the Calculator, the function keys have the following effects:

[F1]	Display the Calculator command menu
[F2]	Request help
[F3]	Unused
[F4]	Undo the most previous delete operation, at the current cursor position
[F5]	Zoom the screen frame on or off.
[F6]	Unused

[F7]	Calculate the square root of the current number
[F8]	Add the current number to the default memory (shown on the top line of the screen frame)
[F9]	Subtract the current number from the default memory (shown on the top line of the screen frame)
[F10]	Memory Recall/Memory Clear

All of the facilities mentioned in this list are described in detail later in this chapter.

OTHER OPERATIONS

In addition to the four basic arithmetic operators and brackets, the Calculator has a number of special operators as follows:

Factorial

To calculate the factorial of a number, type the number immediately followed by an exclamation mark (!). The factorial of the number is immediately displayed in the result window.

Negation

To negate (change the sign) of the number in the result window, press the [Tab] key.

Powers

To calculate powers, use the [^] key. For example, to calculate 2 to the power 8, type:

```
2^8 [Return]
```

Square Root

Press [F7] to calculate the square root of the number in the result window.

Other Roots

To calculate the n'th root of a number x, use the form `x^(1/n)`.

USING THE MEMORIES

The Portfolio Calculator has five memories. Each memory can hold a number taken from the result window. There is always one *default* memory, the number of which (1 to 5) is shown on the top line of the screen frame (between the numeric format and the number of steps.

The memories are accessible by two routes; the function keys [F8], [F9] and [F10], and the **Memories** command in the Calculator command menu. The command menu is described in detail later on in this chapter. For the moment, let's just look at using the function keys to access the default memory.

[F8]	Add the number in the result window to the contents of the default memory
[F9]	Subtract the number in the result window from the contents of the default memory
[F10]	(1st Press) Recall to the result window the contents of the default memory
	(2nd Press) Clear the contents of the default memory.

Try adding a few numbers to the default memory and subtracting a few more. You will notice that the memory in use (the initial default memory is M1) is shown at the top left of the screen frame. This part of the screen frame shows the memories which contain any number other than 0.

Now use [F10] to recall the contents of the default memory, then press [F10] again to clear the contents of the default memory.

For information on changing the default memory and viewing the contents of all five memories, see the description of the **Memories** command later in this chapter.

NUMERIC FORMATS

When you first use the Calculator, the numeric format in use is General. You can also display numbers in fixed decimal, scientific or engineering formats. For more information on numeric formats, see the description of the **Formats** command later in this chapter.

CALCULATING PERCENTAGES

The Portfolio Calculator can be used to calculate percentages in a number of different ways. The simplest of these are to add a percentage to a number or subtract a percentage from a number. You can also determine a mark-up or a mark-down.

It is possible to display not only the final result, but also the amount added or subtracted when using percentages in this way. For further details, see the description of the **Breakdown** command later in this chapter.

To Add a Percentage

A car repair bill is quoted as £250 plus 15% tax. What is the tax-inclusive price?

Press [Esc] until the calculator is clear and the result window shows zero. Now type:

```
250+15% [Return]
```

Note the use of the % (percent) character - hold down [Shift] and press [5].

The screen shows the result 287.5.

To Subtract a Percentage

The car repair shop offers you 20% discount on your bill of £287.50, for being a regular customer. What is the final invoice cost?

Press [Esc] until the calculator is clear and the result window shows zero. Now type:

```
287.5-20% [Return]
```

The screen shows the result 230.

To Calculate Mark-Up

A shop buys Widgets from the manufacturer and agrees to operate at a mark-up of 10% of the sale price. The widgets cost £25.00. What must be the customer price for the shop to make the correct profit?

Press [Esc] until the calculator is clear and the result window shows zero. Now type:

```
25*10% [Return]
```

The screen shows the result 27.7777 ^{r}.

To Calculate Mark-Down

A box of paper from the stationery store costs £10.00 including 15% tax. What is the price not including the tax?

Press [Esc] until the calculator is clear and the result window shows zero. Now type:

```
10/15% [Return]
```

The screen shows the result 8.69565...

THE CALCULATOR COMMANDS

This section describes each of the Calculator commands. To see the Calculator command menu, press [F1]. The screen shows:

```
Calc. 49117
Memories...
Display...
Format...
Breakdown     Off
Printer       Off
Help
```

THE MEMORIES MENU

The **Memories** menu contains a number of commands which control the Calculator's memories. When you select **Memories** from the Calculator command menu, the screen shows:

```
     Memories
Plus (F8)
Minus (F9)
Recall (F10)
Clear...
Show contents
Default        M1
```

The Memories: Plus Command

The **Memories: Plus** command allows you to add the number in the result window to the contents of any of the five memories. When you select **Plus** (or **Minus**, or **Recall** - see below) from the **Memories** menu, the screen shows:

```
Use Memory
Number: 1
```

Type the number of the memory to which the number in the result window should be added, then press [Return].

The Memories: Minus Command

The **Memories: Minus** command allows you to subtract the number in the result window from any of the five memories. When you select **Minus** from the **Memories** menu, type a memory number (1 to 5) and press [Return].

The Memories: Recall Command

The **Memories: Recall** command allows you to recall the contents of any of the five memories. When you select **Recall** from the **Memories** menu, then type a memory number (1 to 5) and press [Return].

The Memories: Clear Command

The **Memories: Clear** command allows you to clear the contents of one or all of the five memories. When you select **Recall** from the **Memories** menu, the screen shows:

```
Clear
All
1
2
3
4
5
```

Select **All** to clear all five memories or select a number to clear just that one memory. Note that when a memory is cleared, its value is simply reset to zero.

When you leave the Calculator and return to DOS, or start some other application, the contents of the memories are preserved until the next time you use the calculator.

The Memories: Show contents Command

The **Memories: Show contents** command allows you view the contents of all five memories at once. When you select **Show contents** from the **Memories** menu, the screen shows a window containing the contents of all five memories.

The Memories: Default Command

The **Memories: Default** command allows you to change the default memory used by [F8] (Memory Plus), [F9] (Memory Minus) and [F10] (Memory Recall/Memory Clear).

When you select **Default** from the **Memories** menu, the screen shows:

```
Default
1
2
3
4
5
```

Select the number of the memory you wish to use as the default, but remember that at any time you can access any of the memories by using the other commands in the **Memories** menu.

THE DISPLAY MENU

When you select **Display** from the Calculator command menu the screen shows:

```
═══ Display ═══
Separators        Off
Decimal point      .
```

The Display: Separators Command

The **Separators** command in the **Display** menu can be used to switch on or off the use of triad separators. The triad separator is a separating character (either a comma or full stop) after every third digit to the left of the decimal point. For example:

10,000,000.0000055	**With** triad separators
10000000.0000055	**Without** triad separators

When the **Display** menu is on the screen, the current state of the separators switch is shown alongside the command. Selecting the command changes the state from On to Off or vice versa.

The Display: Decimal Point Command

The **Decimal Point** command in the **Display** menu is used to select the character used as the decimal point (and therefore the triad separators).

The default decimal point character is the full stop (.), and this character is shown alongside the command in the **Display** menu. To change to the comma (,) just select the command in the usual way.

Note that if you select the full stop as the decimal point, the triad separator (if used) is the comma and vice versa.

THE FORMAT MENU

When you select **Format** from the Calculator command menu, the screen shows a menu of the numeric formats available. The default numeric format is General format. That means that the Calculator will attempt to display the number in the most economic manner it can.

The **Format** menu looks like this:

```
Format
General
Fixed
Scientific
Engineering
```

When you change the display format, only the current number and subsequent numbers are changed to the new format; numbers in the tape remain unchanged.

General Format

The default numeric format is General format. That means that the Calculator will attempt to display the number in the most economic manner it can. If the number is very large or very small, the number is displayed in scientific format (see below).

General format can be reselected after using one of the other formats described below.

Fixed Format

Using fixed format allows the Calculator to display all numbers to a predetermined number of decimal places (between 0 and 12).

For example, here are three numbers as they would be displayed in General format and Fixed format at 4 decimal places:

General Format	Fixed Format
3.1415926535898	3.1416
27.98	27.9800
4	4.0000

When you select Fixed format from the **Format** menu, the screen shows:

```
Dec. places
0 to 12: 2
```

You can now type in the required number of decimal places between the limits shown. When you press [Return], you are returned to the Calculator with the new format in force.

Scientific Format

Scientific format is commonly used for displaying very small or very large numbers. For example, here are three numbers as they would be displayed in full decimal format and scientific format at 3 decimal places:

Number	Scientific Format
0.0000000000268	2.680E-11
252500000	2.525E+08
3.1415926535898	3.142E+00

A number in scientific format consists of a number between 1 (inclusive) and 10 (exclusive), followed by a power. So in the second example above the scientific format number represents:

$$2.525 * 10^8$$

When you select Scientific format from the **Format** menu, the screen shows:

```
Dec. places
0 to 12: 2
```

You can now type in the required number of decimal places between the limits shown. When you press [Return], you are returned to the Calculator with the new format in force.

Engineering Format

This format is very similar to Scientific format as described above, except that the exponent is always a multiple of 3.

THE BREAKDOWN COMMAND

The **Breakdown** command in the Calculator command menu is used to switch on or off the display of percentage breakdowns. When you calculate percentages, as described earlier in this chapter, only the final result is displayed, not the interim figure. For example, one of the examples was to add 15% to 250. The result given is 287.5.

To determine not only the final result, i.e. the figure added to 250 to give the result 287.5, you can use the **Breakdown** command.

When the calculator command menu is displayed, the current setting of the **Breakdown** command is shown alongside the command. If the setting is Off, select **Breakdown**. No further window is displayed on the screen, you are returned immediately to the Calculator display, but the setting is now On.

Press [Esc] until the calculator is clear and the result window shows zero. Now type:

```
250+15% [Return]
```

The screen shows:

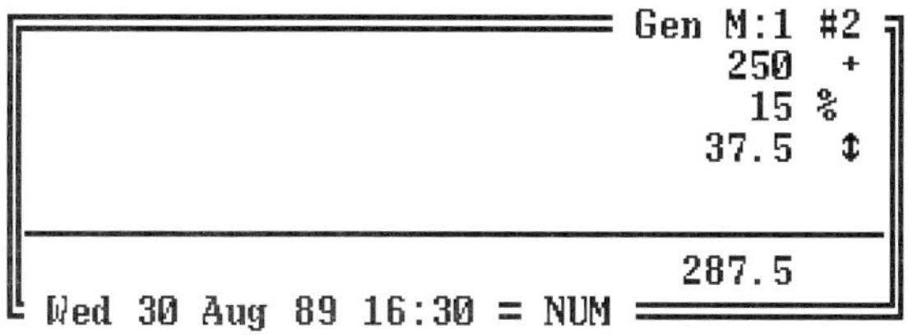

The **Breakdown** command can be used with any percentage operations to determine intermediate results.

THE PRINTER COMMAND

The **Printer** command in the Calculator command menu allows you to direct all output from the Calculator to a printer. See also the section in chapter 9 under the heading PREPARING TO PRINT.

The current printer setting is shown in the Calculator command menu alongside the command. When you select **Printer** from the command menu, the setting is changed from On to Off or vice versa.

When the printer setting is On, all steps in the current calculation are output to the destination (printer or file) set under the Setup option as described in chapter 9. Output is sent to the printer every time you press [Return].

THE HELP COMMAND

The Portfolio has two built-in help systems. The first is accessible when using the application programs - just press [F2] (hold down [Fn] and press [2]). This system gives help on the keyboard, clipboard, undeleting and the function keys.

The second help system is available from the main command menu in each of the application programs, where the last command is **Help**.

When you select Help from the Calculator's main command menu, the screen shows the start of a text file giving hints and reminders on the various features of the Calculator.

You can read through the text file by pressing the [↑] and [↓] keys. To return from the help file to the Calculator menu, press [Esc].

7

THE DIARY

The Portfolio has a built-in Calendar and Diary for keeping track of your appointments and schedules. You can use the Diary to store details of appointments, schedules and times of events.

You can search the Diary for a particular piece of text, perhaps a name or a place. You can make entries repeat every day, week-day, week, month or year; you don't have to enter the time of your regular squash game, it is always there, unless you decide otherwise. You can move appointments around in the Diary as your plans change. You can even set an alarm on any appointment, to remind you in case you forget.

THE FIRST SCREEN

When you start the Diary for the first time, the screen shows:

```
 C:DIARY.DRY ======================= 0
1990   Sun Mon Tue Wed Thu Fri Sat
        29  30  31   1   2   3   4
Aug:     5   6   7   8   9  10  11
        12  13  14  15  16  17  18
        19  20  21  22  23  24  25
        26  27  28  29  30  31   1
 Thu 09 Aug 90 10:30 ===============
```

As usual in the applications, the top line of the frame shows the current file name, **diary.dry**. The top right of the frame shows the number of entries in the current diary file - initially zero. Again, just like in the other applications, press [F5] (hold down [Fn] and press 5) to remove the screen frame.

The screen shows a calendar, just like an ordinary flip-over calendar. The difference is that this one is more like a scroll than a series of monthly blocks. You can use the cursor keys to move around the calendar to any date.

MOVING AROUND THE CALENDAR

Initially the cursor is flashing on today's date. Try moving the cursor a few weeks into the future. Press [↓] a few times and see how the calendar scrolls. Now press the [→] key a few times and watch the cursor move a day at a time into the future.

Back To The Present

With all of this moving around, it is useful to be able to move straight back to today's date, without having to plough back over the calendar the way you came. To return the cursor to today, just press the [Home] key ([Fn] [←]).

When the calendar is displayed, the Diary is in *Calendar mode*. In a moment you will see how to move from Calendar mode into *Diary mode*. The Calendar is always there and is always the first thing you see when you start the Diary from the applications menu or DOS. Similarly, when you leave the Diary itself, you always leave via the Calendar; one press of [Esc] takes you up from the Diary into the Calendar and another press of [Esc] takes you back to the place you were when you started the Diary.

INTO THE DIARY

Press [Home] to return the cursor to today and then press [Return]. This takes you from Calendar mode into Diary mode. (To return from Diary mode to Calendar mode, press [Esc].) The screen shows:

```
╔ C:DIARY.DRY ══════════════════════ 0 ══╗
║──────────────── Thu 09 Aug 1990  10:30 ║
║                                        ║
║                                        ║
╚ Thu 09 Aug 90 10:30 ══════════════ INS ╝
```

The screen is now divided into two areas. The upper part is the *entry window*. It is here that you enter your appointments and other information. The lower part of the screen shows the appointments you have entered, the dates in which they fall and any repeat or alarm settings.

The line between the entry window and the lower part of the screen is the *date-line*. This shows the current *Diary date* and *Diary time*. **Note that these are different to the real date and time set in the Portfolio's clock/calendar**. Initially the two times will be the same, but you can change the Diary date and Diary time as you move around the Diary. The real date and time are displayed on the bottom line of the screen frame, where the time is updated every minute.

TYPING IN APPOINTMENTS

In Diary mode there are a number of ways of entering appointments and changing the current date, as follows:

- type an appointment at the current time
- set a new time
- type a new time with an appointment
- set a new date
- type a new date with a date header

Typing an Appointment at the Current Time

The Diary date and Diary time are shown on the date-line running across the middle of the screen. This is like the header on a page of a paper diary. If you type an entry now, it will be entered in the Diary at that date and time. For example, type:

`Neville's Birthday [Return]`

As you type, the text appears in the entry window. When you press [Return], the screen shows:

```
C:DIARY.DRY ========================== 1 ≈

─────────────── Thu 09 Aug 1990   10:30
 09 Aug 1990 Thu
>  10:30 Neville's Birthday


Thu 09 Aug 90 10:30 ================ INS
```

The Diary has inserted above the text a *date header*; a line which shows just the date of the following one or more entries. Also, at the start of the Diary entry just typed, the Diary has inserted the time of the appointment. If you now type:

```
Remember birthday card! [Return]
```

The screen shows:

```
╔ C:DIARY.DRY ═══════════════════════ 2 ≈ ╗
║
║──────────── Thu 09 Aug 1990  10:30
║ 09 Aug 1990 Thu
║>   10:30 Neville's Birthday
║    10:30 Remember birthday card!
║
╚ Thu 09 Aug 90 10:30 ══════════════ INS ╝
```

The second line of text has been inserted after the first, but the two entries have the same time. Note the pointer at the start of the first entry at the current time, at the left of the screen. Note also that the changed file symbol has appeared at the top right of the screen and that the number of appointments in the current Diary file is being recorded.

Setting a New Time

If you keep on typing appointment messages, they will all appear at the same Diary time. However, you will usually need a different time for each appointment, so you need to be able to change the current Diary time.

In the examples above the Diary time is 10:30. To change the Diary time to, for example, 12:00, type:

```
12:00 [Return]
```

The screen shows:

```
╔ C:DIARY.DRY ═══════════════════════ 2 ≈ ╗
║
║──────────── Thu 09 Aug 1990  12:00
║ 09 Aug 1990 Thu
║    10:30 Neville's Birthday
║>   10:30 Remember birthday card!
║
╚ Thu 09 Aug 90 10:30 ══════════════ INS ╝
```

Note that the new Diary time is shown on the date-line; the Diary date remains the same (for the moment - see below). Now if type:

```
Lunch with Neville [Return]
```

The appointment is given the new Diary time. The screen shows:

```
C:DIARY.DRY ══════════════════════════ 3 ≈
────────────── Thu 09 Aug 1990  12:00
 09 Aug 1990 Thu
   10:30 Neville's Birthday
   10:30 Remember birthday card!
>  12:00 Lunch with Neville
Thu 09 Aug 90 10:30 ════════════ INS
```

Typing a New Time with an Appointment

In the two examples above we typed a new time to set the Diary time and then typed an appointment entry. Instead of the two operations, we could have entered the new time and the appointment together. Try this example. Type:

```
16:00 Take aspirin [Return]
```

The Diary time is immediately changed to the time given (note that the 24 hour clock is used) and the appointment inserted. You can use either a full stop or a colon to separate the hour and minutes. The screen shows:

```
C:DIARY.DRY ══════════════════════════ 4 ≈
────────────── Thu 09 Aug 1990  16:00
   10:30 Neville's Birthday
   10:30 Remember birthday card!
   12:00 Lunch with Neville
>  16:00 Take aspirin
Thu 09 Aug 90 10:30 ════════════ INS
```

Setting a New Date

To change the Diary date, just type in a new date. For example, type:

```
2/9/90 [Return]
```

The Diary date now changes to the date entered. The Diary time remains the same. You can use either a slash (/) or a hyphen (-) to separate the day month and year.

The screen now shows:

```
C:DIARY.DRY ========================= 4 ≈

─────────────── Sun 02 Sep 1990  16:00
    10:30 Neville's Birthday
    10:30 Remember birthday card!
    12:00 Lunch with Neville
>   16:00 Take aspirin
 Thu 09 Aug 90 10:30 =============== INS
```

Remember, whatever the Diary date and Diary time, shown on the date-line across the middle of the screen, the **current** date and time are shown on the bottom line of the screen frame.

Date Formats

The date format must follow that specified in your **config.sys** file as described in chapter 4. To use the British format dd/mm/yy, your **config.sys** file must contain the line:

```
country=044
```

See chapter 4 for more information on the **config.sys** file.

Typing a New Date with a Date Header

If a particular date has some special significance - rather than just some time on that day - you can enter a date header. For example, 18 August is Jo's birthday, so you could type:

```
18/8/90 JO'S BIRTHDAY [Return]
```

The screen shows:

```
C:DIARY.DRY ══════════════════════ 5 ≈
──────────────── Sat 18 Aug 1990  16:00
    10:30 Remember birthday card!
    12:00 Lunch with Neville
    16:00 Take aspirin
> 18 Aug 1990 Sat JO'S BIRTHDAY
 Thu 09 Aug 90 10:30 ═════════════ INS
```

You can now enter appointments for that day or just leave it as a date with a date header.

Now enter a few more dates and appointments until you are really familiar with the way the Diary works.

MOVING AROUND THE DIARY

You can move the cursor around the Diary file simply by using the [↑] and [↓] keys. The list of date headers and appointments scroll up and down accordingly. Remember though that the Diary date and Diary time are always as shown on the date-line across the middle of the screen - the pointer at the left of the screen does not necessarily indicate the Diary date or time.

To move around the file a little more quickly, the following keys may be used:

[Ctrl] [A]	Move to the start of the file (the first appointment)
[Ctrl] [Z]	Move to the end of the file (the last appointment)
[Ctrl] [U]	Move to the previous cursor position
[Ctrl] [→]	Move one word right (while editing)
[Ctrl] [←]	Move one word left (while editing)

[Home]	Move to the appointment nearest the current date and time
[End]	Move to the end of the line (while editing)
[Return]	Change from Calendar to Diary mode
[Esc]	Change from Diary to Calendar mode.

THE FUNCTION KEYS

In the Diary, the function keys have the following effects:

[F1]	Display the Diary command menu
[F2]	Request help
[F3]	View the clipboard menu
[F4]	Undo the most previous delete operation, at the current cursor position
[F5]	Zoom the screen frame on or off
[F6] to [F10]	Unused.

DELETING ENTRIES

To delete any appointment, first use the [↑] or [↓] keys to move the pointer to the entry. When you are sure that this is the appointment to be deleted, just press [Del/Ins]. Both the time and the text alongside are removed and the following appointments moved up to close the gap.

If the deleted appointment is the only appointment in that day, the date header will also be removed **unless** the date header has text of its own (like the JO'S BIRTHDAY header earlier on in this chapter).

You can delete a date header with text in the same way as you would delete an appointment; move the pointer to it and press [Del/Ins].

Undeleting Entries

If you delete the wrong entry, just press [F4] (undelete) to undelete the whole appointment intact.

EDITING ENTRIES

To change the text of an appointment, move the pointer to the entry to be edited and press [Return]. The text of the entry (without the time) is copied up to the entry window. You can now edit the text in the usual way. Press [Return] when the entry reads correctly. The entry is then copied back down into the list of appointments.

You can edit date headers in exactly the same way as appointments.

MOVING ENTRIES

To move a Diary entry from one day to another, but keeping the same time, first delete the entry as described above by pressing the [Del/Ins] key. Now move the pointer to the day where the entry should appear and press [F4] to undelete the entry. The appointment is correctly placed in the list of appointments, according to its time.

If you want to move an entry to a day which currently has no appointments, first change the Diary date to the date you want the appointment to appear (just type that date and press [Return]). Now press [F4] to undelete the appointment.

Alternatively you can use the **Move** command described later in this chapter. The **Move** command also allows you to change the time of an entry.

REPEATING ENTRIES

You decide to go for a three mile run every week-day evening at 7:30pm (19:30). You want to enter the reminder in the Diary, but you don't want to have to enter the same item day after day. The answer is to use the **Repeat** command, described later in this chapter.

The **Repeat** command allows you to make any appointment repeat in the Diary every day, week-day, week, month or year. All you have to do is type the entry once and set the repeater. The Diary does the rest.

SETTING ALARMS

The problem with a conventional diary is that having written in an appointment for next week, unless you refer to your Diary fairly constantly, the appointment can still be forgotten.

The good thing about the Portfolio Diary is that it can remind you of any or all of the appointments you type in. You can set an audible alarm on any appointment which will sound when the Portfolio's clock/calendar reaches that date and time.

You can also use the alarms on repeating entries, so your Portfolio reminds you of your three mile run every week-day evening.

NOTE: The important thing to remember about the Portfolio's Diary alarms is that only alarms set in the file **diary.dry**, stored in the directory called **\system** will be sounded. This is the only Diary file which the Portfolio checks for alarms.

If you set alarms in a Diary file with any other file name, **they will not sound**.

When you use the Diary for the first time, the default file name is **diary.dry**. It is recommended that, at least until you are really familiar with the Portfolio and the way it works, you stay with this one Diary file.

See also the description of the **Alarms** command later in this chapter.

THE DIARY COMMANDS

This section describes each of the Diary commands. To see the Diary command menu, press [F1]. The screen shows:

```
Diary 30466
Files
Search
Move
Repeat
Alarm
Help
```

THE FILES MENU

When you select **Files** from the Diary command menu, the screen shows:

```
Files
New
Load...
Save as...
Merge...
Print
```

The use of the Files commands is similar in each of the file-based applications. A full description of using these commands can be found in chapter 3 under the heading THE FILES COMMANDS. This section gives a brief round-up of the description found there.

The Files: New Command

If you have made any changes to the current file since it was last saved, the file changed symbol will be shown at the upper right corner of the screen frame. If you then select the **Files: New** command, the Portfolio prompts you to save the file, complete with its changes. The screen shows:

```
Save Current?
Yes
No
```

Select **Yes** to save the file under the current file name (shown on the top line of the screen frame), or select **No** to discard the current file **including any changes you have made since the last time the file was saved**.

The Files: Load Command

The **Files: Load** command is used to load an existing file from a drive into an application. A copy of the file is made from the original which is stored on the drive. Loading a file does not have any effect on the original file, unlike saving (see the **Files: Save as** command below).

When you select the **Files: Load** command, the Portfolio prompts you to enter the name of the file you want to load. The screen shows:

```
Load
Name: C:\SYSTEM\DIARY.DRY
```

The default file name (shown in the dialogue box) is always the file name most recently used by the current application program. If the current file name is, for example, **diary.dry**, that is the file name offered by the dialogue box. You now have four options:

1. Press [Return] to load the file shown in the dialogue box

2. Edit the file name to that of the file you want to load

3. Press the [*] key to see all files from the current application

4. Press the [:] key to see a list of all of the files and sub-directories found in the current directory.

Note that item 3 in the list above is the equivalent of typing *.* (see chapter 4 for more details of this in relation to DOS). You can also type a new, full path name with or without a file name, including wildcards, just like those used in DOS.

The Files: Save as Command

The **Files: Save as** command is used to save a copy of the current file under the same or a different name on any drive. If there is already a copy of the file under the name you use, **the old copy will be overwritten by the new copy**, so make sure you are not losing some vital information by using an existing file name.

If you save a new copy of a file under a name different from that of the original file, then the original file will be unaffected when you make your new copy.

For further details of the way in which file names are given, refer to the section above under the heading **The Files: Load Command**.

Note: The Golden Rule when using any type of computer is this - and there are no exceptions:

Always make a back-up copy of any file which is really important.

You can make a copy onto a memory card or via the optional communications link to a desk-top pc. Then if disaster strikes, you still have a copy of your important data.

The Files: Merge Command

Sometime it is useful to merge one file with another, to make a single larger file. For example, if you have two diaries, one for personal appointments and another for business appointments, you can do so using the **Files: Merge** command.

When you use the **Merge** command, the selected file is combined with the current file. The timed entries are sorted into chronological order and placed into the appropriate date slots.

When you select **Merge** from the **Files** menu, the screen shows:

```
Merge
Name:
```

You now have three options:

1. Press the [*] key to see all files from the current application

2. Press the [:] key to see a list of all of the files and sub-directories found in the current directory

3. Type the name of the Diary file you want to merge with the current file.

Note that item 1 in the list above is the equivalent of typing *.* (see chapter 4 for more details of this in relation to DOS). You can also type a new, full path name with or without a file name, including wildcards, just like those used in DOS.

When you have selected a file, the file is combined with the current file and you can continue editing the new, combined file. The current file name is not changed during this operation, and the original copies of the first file and the merged file are unaffected.

The Files: Print Command

The **Print** command is used to print the contents of the current file to a printer (serial or parallel) or to a file on a drive. For more information on the destination of your printed output, including the page length, margins and so on, see the section under the heading PREPARING TO PRINT in chapter 9.

When the **Files: Print** command is selected, the screen shows the message **Printing...** while the whole file is printed. Note that the margins and page length of the printed output are taken from the current settings made in the Portfolio's Setup facility. See chapter 9 for further details of Setup.

Printing With Postscript

Many offices now use laser printers instead of the old daisy-wheel or dot-matrix printers. Laser printers are quieter than impact printers and often a great deal faster. The print quality is very high and a great number of print styles are available. Some of the most impressive of these printers use the page description language PostScript.

The Portfolio's Diary is not equipped to drive these laser printers to the limit but, with a little effort, the Portfolio can use them to very good effect. In chapter 13 you will find details of a disk containing a suite of PostScript programs which enable you to print Diary files, business graphs and a variety of special type styles from the Portfolio.

THE SEARCH COMMAND

When you have typed in a large number of appointments, you may want to search the Diary for a particular word or phrase. For example, you have made a lunch appointment with Mike & Jane, but can't remember when.

When you select the **Search** command from the Diary command menu, the screen shows:

```
Search
For:
```

You can now type **Mike** or **Mike & Jane** or **JANE** and press any of the following keys:

[Return]	search in the last direction used (initially forwards)
[↑]	search backwards in the Diary
[↓]	search forwards in the Diary.

If the text is found, the cursor is moved to that appointment in the file. It doesn't matter if you type the text in upper or lower case letters, case is ignored.

You can search for the next occurrence of the given text in the same direction, perhaps for the next lunch date with Mike & Jane, either by selecting the Search command again and just pressing [Return], or you can just type [Ctrl] [S] (hold down [Ctrl] and press [S]. The cursor then moves to the next occurrence of the text, if any. If a given piece of text is not found, the message **String not found** is displayed. Press [Esc] to cancel the message.

THE MOVE COMMAND

We saw earlier how you can move an appointment from one day to another, using the [Del/Ins] key to delete the appointment and then the [F4] key to undelete that appointment on a different day. A rather better way of moving an appointment from one time or date (or both) to another is to use the **Move** command.

To move an appointment, first move the pointer to that appointment by pressing the [↑] or [↓] key. When you select the **Move** command from the Diary command menu, the screen shows:

```
═══ Move ═══
Time: 10:30
```

You can now either type a new time for the appointment or edit the time offered in the window. When you press [Return], the screen shows:

```
═══ Move ═══
Date: 10/08/89
```

You can now either type a new date for the appointment or edit the date offered in the window. Press [Return] to complete the move.

THE REPEAT MENU

We saw earlier in this chapter that any appointment in the Diary can be made to repeat on a daily, week-daily, weekly, monthly or yearly basis. The repeat facility is controlled using the commands in the **Repeat** menu. When you select **Repeat** from the Diary command menu, the screen shows:

```
═ Repeat ═
Daily
Weekly
Non-Weekend
Monthly
Yearly
Clear
```

You can now select any of the repeat periods or **Clear**. When you select, for example, **Daily**, a **d** is displayed alongside the current appointment. That appointment will now be repeated and appear in the Diary for every day until the repeater is cleared.

When a repeater is set, you don't get a string of previous copies of the appointment left behind as the days or weeks go by, the previous versions are cleared up automatically. In fact the repeating appointment is just moved from period to period by the Diary.

If you have selected a daily repeat for an appointment and then decide to change this to week-daily, just select the new repeat while the pointer is alongside the appointment. Any previous repeat setting is cancelled and replaced by the new one.

Repeating appointments may also have an alarm setting, so the repeating appointment sounds an alarm every time it becomes due.

The Repeat: Monthly Command

The **Monthly** repeat setting can of course be set to repeat on any day of the month. However, if you set a monthly repeat on, for example, 31 August, when the appointment then appears in September, there is no 31st day, so the appointment appears on the 30th. The appointment will stay on the 30th day of the month until February, when it will again appear on the last day (28 or 29). The appointment then stays on that day of the month throughout the year.

The Repeat: Clear Command

To remove any repeater setting, move the pointer to the appropriate entry and select **Clear** from the **Repeat** menu.

THE ALARM COMMAND

NOTE: The first and most important thing to remember about the Portfolio's Diary alarms is that only alarms set in the file **diary.dry**, stored in the directory called **\system** will be sounded. **This is the only Diary file which the Portfolio checks for alarms.**

If you set alarms in a Diary file with any other file name, **they will not sound**. Alarms can only sound when you have saved the file **diary.dry** and left the Diary. Alarms will not sound while you are using the Diary.

When you use the Diary for the first time, the default file name is **diary.dry**. It is recommended that, at least until you are really familiar with the Portfolio and the way it works, you stay with this one Diary file.

Now let's look at how to set an alarm. First move the pointer to the appointment you would like to be reminded of. Press [F1] to see the Diary command menu, and select **Alarm**. You are immediately returned to the Diary display with a 'music' character shown alongside the appropriate entry. For example, the screen might show:

```
╔ C:DIARY.DRY ═══════════════════════ 4 ≈ ╗
║                                          ║
╟──────────── Thu 09 Aug 1990   16:00      ║
║ 09 Aug 1990 Thu                          ║
║    10:30 Neville's Birthday              ║
║▸ ♫ 10:30 Remember birthday card!         ║
║    12:00 Lunch with Neville              ║
╚ Thu 09 Aug 90 10:32 ═════════════════════╝
```

Cancelling an Alarm

Now you can leave the Diary, use some other application, even switch the Portfolio off, but when the time of the alarmed appointment becomes due, an alarm will sound.

The text of the appointment is shown on the screen in a window while the alarm sounds. Press any key to silence the alarm, then press [Esc] to cancel the message and return to the activity taking place before the alarm sounded.

See also the section below under the heading Silent Alarms.

Deleting an Alarm

To delete an alarm before the alarm becomes due, move the pointer to the alarmed appointment and select the **Alarm** command from the Diary command menu. The 'music' character is removed and the alarm setting is deleted.

Silent Alarms

You might be going into a meeting and don't want to be disturbed by the Diary alarms. You can silence all Diary alarms by using the **Sound** command in the Portfolio's Setup facility (see chapter 9).

The text of an alarmed appointment is still displayed on the screen at the appropriate time, but no sound is made. The alarm is cleared in the usual way by pressing [Esc].

THE HELP COMMAND

The Portfolio has two built-in help systems. The first is accessible when using the application programs - just press [F2]. This system gives help on the keyboard, clipboard, undeleting and the function keys.

The second help system is available from the main command menu in each of the application programs, where the last command is **Help**.

When you select **Help** from the Diary's main command menu, the screen shows:

```
==== Help ====
Menus
File handling
```

The first menu option gives help on the Diary command menu and its sub-menus. The second option gives specific help on the use of the **Files** commands, concerned with loading and saving files.

In each of the help options, the help is in the form of a text file which you can read through by pressing the [↑] and [↓] keys. To return from one of the help files to the Help menu, press [Esc].

8

THE EDITOR

THE BASICS

The Portfolio's Editor is a text-editing program. It can be used to type in text in much the same way as you would type text on a typewriter. The Editor, however, offers many facilities not found on an ordinary typewriter.

How It Works

When you type on a typewriter, the line fills up until the right margin is reached - then the bell rings. You push back the carriage and carry on typing on the next line. At the end of the paragraph you give two carriage returns.

Typing in the editor is rather similar, but the waiting for the bell and pushing back the platen is all gone. As you type, the line fills up until you reach the right margin. When you type a word which will not fit on the current line, it is automatically pushed down on to the next line where you can carry on typing. You just type away at full speed and the Editor does the rest, breaking lines where necessary.

At the end of a paragraph, just like on the typewriter, you press the [Return] key (a *carriage return*) twice.

If you decide you want to change some of the text you have typed, you can just go back to that part of the document and either type over the old text with the new, or delete text, or add more text, or correct your spelling or just about anything else.

If you have written a long document and you want to look for the paragraph where John is mentioned, you can search for the word John. You can even search for and replace any text with any other text.

There are many more facilities available within the Editor and these are described in detail in the following pages.

THE FIRST SCREEN

When you first select the Editor from the applications menu, the screen shows:

```
╔ C:UNNAMED.TXT ══════ L:1 C:1 M:37 ══╗
║<                                    ║
║                                     ║
║                                     ║
║                                     ║
╚ Thu 09 Aug 90 10:30 ════════════════╝
```

As usual in the applications, the top line of the frame shows the current file name, **unnamed.txt**, and the position of the *cursor* in the current document. Again, just like in the other applications, press [F5] (hold down [Fn] and press 5) to remove the screen frame.

The cursor is the flashing block which shows where your next typed text will appear. Of course, because you have just started the Editor for the first time, the document

unnamed.txt is empty, so the cursor is at the top of the screen on the left hand side. If there is no character under the flashing cursor, the Word Wrap feature is turned off; press [F1] then press [W]. This turns the word wrap feature on again. Don't worry too much about this just now, all will be explained later.

The Editor automatically gives files the extension **.txt** (see chapters 2 and 4 for more details of files and file extensions).

TYPING SOME TEXT

As an example, try typing the following text into the Editor:

```
To fight against the shoddy design of
goods by which our fellow-men are
surrounded becomes a moral duty.
(Nikolaus Pevsner).
```

Remember, you just type the text from start to finish, the Editor arranges the words on the screen. The screen now looks like this:

```
C:UNNAMED.TXT ══════ L:4 C:20 M:37 ≈
To fight against the shoddy design
of goods by which our fellow-men are
surrounded becomes a moral duty.
(Nikolaus Pevsner).<


Thu 09 Aug 90 10:30 ═══════════════
```

The Editor allows you to type continuously, and arranges the words for you on the screen. This is because the Editor automatically *word-wraps* the text. If a word will not fit on the current line, it is moved down to the next line and so on.

The length of the line which the Editor works to is set by the **Right Margin** command. The right margin can be set at anything from 5 to 250 characters.

However, if you have the word wrap feature switched off, the text will all stay on one line and will not be automatically broken at the right margin.

This all boils down to the following:

- If you want to type an ordinary document using automatic word wrap, switch word wrap on (see the **Word Wrap** command later in this chapter)
- When word wrap in on, the end of each paragraph (a carriage return) is visible on screen like this: <
- When you print out a document, the line length on the paper is taken from the right margin setting and any left margin set in the Portfolio's Setup facility (see chapter 9).

All of the Editor commands mentioned here are described later in this chapter.

EDITING THE TEXT

You will, of course, have noticed that I misquoted the great Nikolaus Pevsner. In his book 'Industrial Art in England' he says, '...the shoddy design of **those** goods...'. So let's go back and insert the missing word.

Inserting Text

Set the keyboard into Insert mode by holding down the [Shift] key and pressing [Del/Ins] (the bottom line of the screen frame now shows INS to denote Insert mode). Now use the cursor keys to go back up to the start of the word **goods**. Type the word **those** followed by a space. The screen now shows:

```
C:UNNAMED.TXT ═════ L:2 C:11 M:37 ≈
To fight against the shoddy design
of those goods by which our fellow-
men are surrounded becomes a moral
duty. (Nikolaus Pevsner).<


Thu 09 Aug 90 10:30 ══════════════
```

Deleting Text

You might want to delete some part of the text in the file. There are two main keys used to delete small amounts of text; the [Del/Ins] key and the [BS] key.

- Use the [Del/Ins] key to delete the character under the cursor
- Use the [BS] (back space) key to delete the character to the left of the cursor when the keyboard is in Insert mode.

Using these two keys is fine for deleting small amounts of text, but larger amounts need a quicker method. For this reason, there are a number of keyboard shortcuts which allow you to delete whole words and lines at a time:

Key Press	**Action**
[Ctrl] [B]	Delete back to start of line
[Ctrl] [E]	Delete to end of line
[Ctrl] [L]	Delete whole of current line
[Ctrl] [W]	Delete word to right of cursor
[Ctrl] [BS]	Delete word to left of cursor

These shortcuts make it much easier to delete large blocks of text. Alternatively you can use the **Cut** option within the clipboard (see chapter 3 and the section below under the heading Moving Text). The clipboard allows you to cut blocks of text in a single unit which can then either be discarded or put into another file.

Undeleting Text

When you delete text using the [Del/Ins] key, the [BS] key or any of the keyboard shortcuts mentioned above, all of the deleted text is saved in a file called **undelete.dat**. This file may be saved when you leave the applications, according to the setting made in Setup (see chapter 9 and the end of chapter 3 for details of Setup and undeleting respectively).

The basis of the Portfolio's ability to undelete information is that when you press the [F4] key, the most recently deleted item of information is placed in the current file at the current cursor position. That item of information might be a single character, it might be a word or it might be a whole line of information. If the information came from the Address Book, it might be a whole record, or from the Worksheet a block of cells. Any information taken from any type of file can be undeleted into any other type of file.

So you don't have to worry; if you have just deleted ten lines of matchless prose by repeatedly pressing [Ctrl] [L], you can retrieve every word pressing [F4] an equal number of times.

Moving Text

One major feature of any text editor or word processor is the ability to move blocks of text around within a document and from one document to another. The Portfolio's Editor allows you to do this using the clipboard.

In the text we typed in earlier, we might want to move the credit up to the top line, changing the text to read:

```
Nikolaus Pevsner said, "To fight against
the shoddy design of those goods by
```

```
which our fellow-men are surrounded
becomes a moral duty".
```

First move the cursor to the start of the credit, on the space before the opening bracket. Press the [Del/Ins] key twice to remove the space and the bracket. Now press [F3] to use the clipboard.

The screen shows:

```
Clipboard
Cut
Store
Paste
Mark
```

Select **Mark** to mark the start of the block of text you want to put into the clipboard. Now move the cursor to the end of ‘Pevsner’. Press [Del/Ins] twice more to remove the bracket and the final full stop.

Press [F3] again to see the clipboard menu. This time select **Cut** to cut out the text between the cursor and the mark. The text ‘Nikolaus Pevsner’ is cut out of the document and into the clipboard. You can now move the cursor to the top of the document by pressing [Ctrl] [A].

Press [F3] again to see the clipboard menu and select **Paste**; the whole contents of the clipboard, i.e. the text ‘Nikolaus Pevsner’, is pasted into the document at the current cursor position.

Now you can add in the ‘said, “’ at the appropriate position to complete the changes.

As we saw earlier in this chapter, you can move small amounts of text from one place to another by using the Portfolio’s undelete facility ([F4]), but for larger blocks of text, the clipboard is the preferred way. See chapter 3 for full details of using the clipboard.

Saving the File

When you have made your changes, you will want to save the file so that it can be recalled for later use. Press [F1] to see the Editor main command menu, and select **Files**. From the **Files** menu, select **Save as**. The screen shows:

```
Save
Name: UNNAMED.TXT
```

Just type a new name for the file, without the file extension - **.txt** is automatically added by the Editor. For example, type:

```
pevsner [Return]
```

The file is saved immediately to drive **c:** as **pevsner.txt**.

See chapter 3 for full details on saving and loading files; see also chapters 2 and 4 for further details of files and directories.

MOVING AROUND

So far you have just used the cursor keys on their own for moving the cursor around the screen. That is fine for such a small document as this, but on larger files, moving around by a character at a time can be rather trying. For this reason, there are a number of keyboard shortcuts which allow you to move the cursor around a file much more quickly:

Key Press	Action
[Ctrl] [A]	Go to start of current file
[Ctrl] [U]	Return to previous cursor position
[Ctrl] [Z]	Go to end of current file
[Ctrl] [→]	Move cursor one word to right
[Ctrl] [←]	Move cursor one word to left

[Fn] [←]	Go to start of current line
[Fn] [→]	Go to end of current line
[Fn] [↑]	Move cursor up 2/3 one screen
[Fn] [↓]	Move cursor down 2/3 one screen

Try some of these key combinations and you will see how useful they can be.

THE EDITOR AT WORK

At the start of this chapter, we just saw a few of the things that the Editor could do. This section gives a few more and shows how the Editor, used together with the other Portfolio applications, can be used to the full.

The most obvious use for the Editor is as a means of producing documents, letters, reports, memos and so on, but there are other uses too. The Editor is the ideal tool for creating and maintaining a general personal memo file - a list of things to do. Create a file called **notepad.txt** and use it to make notes, reminders, lists and the like. As items become redundant they can be deleted from the file. The file can also be printed at any time.

The Editor & The Address Book

Perhaps your Address Book file on the Portfolio contains the name and address of someone to whom you want to write a letter. There's no need to type the address out in full at the head of the letter, why not copy it from the Address Book using the Portfolio's ability to undelete information?

- First start the Address Book in the usual way and find the appropriate record in your name and address file (in Line mode)
- Press [Del/Ins] to delete the current record

- Press [Esc] to escape from the Address Book and press [N] (No you don't want to save the Address Book file less one record)
- Start the Editor in the usual way and start a new file with the **Files: New** command
- Press [F4] to undelete the record from the Address Book into the current text file.

You can then delete any telephone number which appears on the first line of the record and your address is all done. Using this method of inserting an address is quicker and easier than typing it out again, and, provided your name and address file is correct, the addresses in your letters will always be correct too.

The Editor & The Diary

The Portfolio's undelete and clipboard facilities allow you to type text into an Editor file and then transfer it into a Diary file. This means you can build a Diary file by typing the text in as straight text, adding alarms and repeats as necessary by the simple inclusion of a single character. When you have planned your day (week, month, year) you just transfer the lot into the Diary via the clipboard.

For example, clear the Editor by pressing [F1] [F] (for the **Files** menu) and [N] (**New** file). Now type the following, pressing [Return] at the end of each line:

```
18/08/90 BIRTHDAY GIRL
y@ 07:00 Birthday Breakfast
11:00 Meet the managing director
@ 13:00 Lunch with stockbroker
15:00 Everything stops for tea
n@ 19:00 G&T (Ice, no lemon)
20:00 Dinner (remember Champagne)
19/08/90
06:00 Take aspirin
06:00 Stay in bed
```

The first line forms a date header with text. The date should be entered in the format specified by the **country** command in your **config.sys** file. See chapter 4 for more details of the **config.sys** file.

The second line is a yearly repeating entry with an alarm. The @ character denotes an entry with an alarm.

The 11:00, 15:00 and 20:00 entries do not have an alarm setting and do not repeat. The 13:00 appointment has an alarm but does not repeat. The 19:00 reminder repeats every non-weekend day (ie Monday to Friday) and sounds an alarm.

Next comes a plain day header with no following text. The last two entries do not repeat and have no alarms.

When you have typed the entries exactly as shown, move the cursor to the top of the document by typing [Ctrl] [A], copy the whole document into the clipboard as described above and start the Diary in the usual way.

When you enter the Diary, start a new file with the **Files: New** command and then use the clipboard again to paste the text from above into the new Diary file. The screen then looks like this:

```
C:DIARY.DRY ═══════════════════════ 8 ≈
─────────────── Sun 19 Aug 1990  06:00
n♫ 19:00 G&T (Ice, no lemon)
 19 Aug 1990 Sun
▸   06:00 Stay in bed
    06:00 Take aspirin
Thu 09 Aug 90 10:30 ═══════════════════
```

Note that only alarms set within the Diary file **diary.dry** stored in the directory called **\system** will sound. See chapter 7 for further details of using the Diary.

Chapter 15 contains a more complete description of the file formats of all of the Portfolio's applications.

The Editor & the Worksheet

Occasionally you may need to type a letter containing a set of figures. The normal route would be to work out your figures, type the letter and then copy the relevant figures into the letter, one at a time, aligning the figures as best you could.

The Portfolio makes the job a great deal easier. The best way to prepare your figures in the first place is in the Portfolio's Worksheet. You can arrange the figures in a sensible way, with appropriate text headers, currency format display and so on. You can then copy the results into the clipboard and paste a copy into your letter.

There are obvious benefits in terms of getting the figures correct and neatly presented in your letter, but if some of the figures need to change, just change them in the Worksheet and re-copy them to the letter.

CHANGING PRINT STYLE

The Portfolio will allow you to print your files to any type of computer printer. The optional communications adapter plugs into the right side of the Portfolio's casing. You can then plug in a cable to link the Portfolio to your printer and print any of the documents in the computer.

The Editor's **Print** command is described in detail later in this chapter, but this section describes how to insert control codes into your documents which enable the use of various facilities on your printer. For example, most printers can print in a bold or 'emphasised' typeface; some can underline or print in italics. This section also lists control codes for the following printers:

- Epson FX-80
- Diablo 630
- Hewlett Packard LaserJet
- Qume Sprint 11

Typing In the Control Codes

All of the control codes listed here start with the Escape character. This is distinct from the [Esc] key which is often mentioned in this book. The Escape character is part of the Portfolio's character set, just like any other character.

The difference is that the Escape character has no printable form - it can be put in a document and sent to a printer, but it does not make a mark on the page. Instead it is used as a command header. When the printer sees the Escape character, it knows that the next thing it receives will be a print control code.

For example, the Epson FX-80 printer understands that, when it receives the two characters Escape E, it should start printing in emphasised mode. This print mode is used until either the printer is switched off, or the print mode is reset (with another command) to normal.

The Escape character is often represented as the caret character followed by a square bracket like this, ^[. And in fact, if you type those two characters into a document, at first nothing appears after the caret - it is only when you type the left square bracket that the combined character appears. This represents the Escape character.

We can use the text we typed in earlier as an example. Perhaps we want to print the credit, Nikolaus Pevsner, in emphasised type on an Epson FX-80. First move the cursor to the start of Nikolaus, and type a caret followed by a left square bracket, then type [E]. Move to the end of Pevsner and type a caret followed by a square bracket, then type [F] (to switch emphasised print off).

When you print the document the text Nikolaus Pevsner will be printed emphasised.

In all of the following lists of commands, the Escape character is represented by (Esc). There are no spaces between the (Esc) and the other parts of the commands and none should be inserted.

EPSON FX-80 PRINT CONTROLS

(Esc)G	Double Strike On
(Esc)H	Double Strike Off
(Esc)E	Emphasise On
(Esc)F	Emphasise Off
(Esc)W1	Enlarged Print (wide) On
(Esc)W0	Enlarged Print (wide) Off
(Esc)4	Italic On
(Esc)5	Italic Off
(Esc)M	Set Compressed Pitch
(Esc)P	Set Standard Pitch

(Esc)1	Subscript On
(Esc)0	Superscript On
(Esc)T	Sub/Super. Off
(Esc)-1	Underline On
(Esc)-0	Underline Off

DIABLO 630 PRINT CONTROLS

(Esc)M	Auto Justify On
(Esc)O	Bold On (up to end of line or (Esc)& or (Esc)X)
(Esc)W	Shadow Print On (up to end of line or (Esc)& or (Esc)X)
(Esc)&	Bold/Shadow Off
(Esc)X	Cancel WP Modes
(Esc)A	(secondary colour) Italic On
(Esc)B	(primary colour) Italic Off
(Esc)E	Underline on
(Esc)R	Underline off

HEWLETT-PACKARD PRINT CONTROLS

A full description of the font selection commands used by the Hewlett Packard LaserJet is beyond the scope of this book. For more details, refer to your printer's User Manual.

(Esc)(s1S	Italic On
(Esc)(s0S	Italic Off
(Esc)&l1H	Select Main Cassette
(Esc)&l2H	Select Manual Feed

(Esc)&k2S	Set Compressed Pitch
(Esc)&k0S	Set Standard Pitch
(Esc)&d0	Underline On
(Esc)&d@	Underline Off

QUME SPRINT 11 PRINT CONTROLS

(Esc)Kn	Bold Print On (where n is a number from 1 to 4)
(Esc)M	Bold Print Off
(Esc)Q	Shadow Print On
(Esc)R	Shadow Print Off
(Esc)I	Underline On
(Esc)J	Underline Off

PRINTING WITH POSTSCRIPT

Many offices now use laser printers instead of the old daisy-wheel or dot-matrix printers. Laser printers are quieter than impact printers and often a great deal faster. The print quality is very high and a great number of print styles are available. Some of the most impressive of these printers use the page description language PostScript.

The Portfolio's Editor is not equipped to drive these laser printers to the limit but, with a little effort, the Portfolio can use them to very good effect. In chapter 13 you will find a PostScript program which can be used to make the Portfolio drive any PostScript printer, or even a typesetting machine operating at 2400 dots per inch!

There are also details of a disk containing a suite of PostScript programs which enable you to print business graphs and a variety of special type styles from the Portfolio.

THE EDITOR COMMAND MENU

This section describes each of the Editor commands. To view the Editor command menu, press [F1]. The screen shows:

```
Editor 40800
Files...
Search...
Right Margin  37
Word Wrap     On
Mode         INS
Help...
```

The Editor commands are presented in the usual menu format. Some of the options in the menu lead to further menus and options. The full range of options and commands is described below:

THE FILES MENU

When you select **Files** from the Editor command menu, the screen shows:

```
Files
New
Load...
Save as...
Merge...
Print
```

The use of the **Files** commands is very much the same in each of the file-based applications. A full description of using these commands can be found in chapter 3 under the heading THE FILES COMMANDS. This section gives a brief round-up of the description found there.

The Files: New Command

If you have made any changes to the current file since it was last saved, the file changed symbol will be shown at the upper right corner of the screen frame. If you then select the **Files: New** command, the Portfolio prompts you to save the file, complete with its changes. The screen shows:

```
Save Current?
Yes
No
```

Select **Yes** to save the file under the current file name (shown on the top line of the screen frame), or select **No** to discard the current file **including any changes you have made since the last time the file was saved**.

The Files: Load Command

The **Files: Load** command is used to load an existing file from a drive into an application. A copy of the file is made from the original which is stored on the drive - loading a file does not have any effect on the original file, unlike saving (see the **Files: Save as** command below).

When you select the **Files: Load** command, the Portfolio prompts you to enter the name of the file you want to load. The screen shows:

```
Load
Name: C:\TEXT\UNNAMED.TXT
```

The default file name (shown in the dialogue box) is always the file name most recently used by the current application program. If the current file name is, for example, **unnamed.txt**, that is the file name offered by the dialogue box. You now have four options:

1. Press [Return] to load the file shown in the dialogue box

2. Edit the file name to that of the file you want to load

3. Press the [*] key to see all files from the current application

4. Press the [:] key to see a list of all of the files and sub-directories found in the current directory.

Note that item 3 in the list above is the equivalent to typing *.* (see chapter 4 for more details of this in relation to DOS). You can also type a new, full path name with or without a file name, including wildcards, just like those used in DOS.

The Files: Save as Command

The **Files: Save as** command is used to save a copy of the current file under the same or a different name on any drive. If there is already a copy of the file under the name you use, **the old copy will be overwritten by the new copy**, so make sure you are not losing some vital information by using an existing file name.

If you save a new copy of a file under a name different from that of the original file, then the original file will be unaffected when you make your new copy.

For further details of the way in which file names are given, refer to the section above under the heading **The Files: Load Command**.

Note: The Golden Rule when using any type of computer is this - and there are no exceptions:

- **Always make a back-up copy of any file which is really important.**

You can make a copy onto a memory card or via the optional communications link to a desk-top pc. Then if disaster strikes, you have a copy of your important data.

The Files: Merge Command

Sometime it is useful to merge one file with another, to make a single larger file. Of course, if you have typed a letter and you just want to include a few lines from another document, you could just use the clipboard. If, however, you really want to merge two whole documents together, you need the **Files: Merge** command.

When you use the **Merge** command, the selected file is inserted into the current file at the current cursor position, so make sure you are at the correct place in your file before using the command.

When you select **Merge** from the **Files** menu, the screen shows:

```
═══════════════ Merge ═══════════════
 Name:
```

You now have three options:

1. Press the [*] key to see all files from the current application

2. Press the [:] key to see a list of all of the files and sub-directories found in the current directory

3. Type the name of the document you want to merge with the current file.

Note that item 1 in the list above is the equivalent to typing *.* (see chapter 4 for more details of this in relation to DOS).

You can also type a new, full path name with or without a file name, including wildcards, just like those used in DOS.

When you have selected a file, the file is inserted into the current file and you can continue editing the new, combined file. The current file name is not changed during this operation, and the original copies of the first file and the merged file are unaffected.

The Files: Print Command

The **Print** command is used to print the contents of the current file to a printer (serial or parallel) or to a file on a drive. For more information on the destination of your printed output, including the page length, margins and so on, see the section under the heading PREPARING TO PRINT in chapter 9.

When the **Files: Print** command is selected, the screen shows the message **Printing...** while the whole file is printed.

THE SEARCH MENU

When you have typed a long document, you may want to search the file for a particular word or phrase, or go to a particular line in the document. Or even search for one piece of text and replace it with another throughout the file. These are the facilities provided by the **Search** menu.

The Search: Search Command

The **Search** command allows you to search the current file for a given word or phrase. If the given text is found, you can then search for the next occurrence of the text and so on to the end of the file.

When the **Search** command is selected from the **Search** menu, the screen shows:

```
═══ Search ═══
For:
```

You can now type in the text to be found, and press any of the following keys:

[Return]	search in the last direction used (initially forwards)
[↑]	search backwards in the current file
[↓]	search forwards in the current file.

If the text is found, the cursor is moved to that text in the file. It doesn't matter if you type the text in upper or lower case letters, case is ignored. So if you search for the text **OK**, the Editor will stop on **OK** or **joking**.

You can search for the next occurrence of the given text in the same direction either by selecting the Search command again and just pressing [Return], or you can just type [Ctrl] [S] (hold down [Ctrl] and press [S]). The cursor then moves to the next occurrence of the text, if any. If a given piece of text is not found, the message **String not found** is displayed. Press [Esc] to cancel the message.

The Search: Replace Command

Your company has just developed the new Wamdidget Edrificator, which will change the world of motor-cycle maintenance for ever. Your report to the staff mentions the Edrificator on just about every page: A last minute change of plan... the Edrificator is to be renamed the Drific! You need to change the text Edrificator to Drific throughout your document:

Select the **Search: Replace** command. The screen shows:

```
═══ Search ═══
For:
```

Type Edrificator and press [Return]. The screen shows:

```
┌ Replace: EDRIFICA ┐
│ With:             │
└───────────────────┘
```

Type Drific and press [Return]. The first occurrence of Edrificator is replaced. Now press [Ctrl] [R] a number of times to replace all other occurrences of the word. When the last has been replaced, the next [Ctrl] [R] will produce the message **String not found**.

Beware! There is the story of a member of the clergy who started using a computer to prepare orders of service for weddings. He used the Replace function on his computer to replace all occurrences of Ian and Mary with Steve and Susan. That was fine when the new orders were printed out, except that the prayer now read 'Hail Susan, full of grace...'. A computer will do what you tell it - no more, no less.

The Search: Goto Command

If you have a file which you know to be 500 lines long (the current line number is shown in the top edge of the screen frame), you might want to move the cursor to, say, the half way point in the file. The **Search: Goto** command allows you to move the cursor to a given line number.

When you select the **Goto** command, the screen shows:

```
╔═══ Goto ═══╗
║ Line: 1    ║
╚════════════╝
```

The default line number shown in the dialogue box is 1, you can now type the number of the line you want to go to, using the example above, type 250 and press [Return]. The cursor immediately moves to line 250 in your document.

If the number of lines in your document is smaller than the number you type in, the cursor moves to the end of the file.

You can also use the **Search: Goto** command to move a number of lines relative to the current cursor position. Instead of a line number, type a number with a plus or a minus sign and the cursor moves up or down by the given number of lines.

For example, enter +20 and the cursor moves down the document by 20 lines; enter -20 and the cursor moves up the document by 20 lines.

Once you have used **Goto** in this way, you can then use [Ctrl] [G] to repeat the action and step through the document by the same number of lines in the same direction.

THE RIGHT MARGIN COMMAND

When automatic word wrap is switched on, when you type, if a word will not fit on the current line, the line is automatically broken and the word is placed on the next line. The Editor works to the margin set by the **Right Margin** command. The current right margin setting is shown at the top right of the screen frame. The default setting is 37 characters.

When you select **Right Margin** from the Editor command menu, the screen shows:

```
==== Right Margin ====
 Set to (5-250):
```

You can now type the number of characters you want your line length to be, then press [Return]. Note that most typing paper is around 80 characters wide and the screen of the Portfolio is 40 characters wide (less 2 for the screen frame - press [F5] to remove the frame).

You are immediately returned to your document. If word wrap is switched on, the text is reformatted to fit within the new right margin.

Note also that:

- If you want to type an ordinary document using automatic word wrap, switch word wrap on (using the Word Wrap command, see below)
- When word wrap in on, the end of each paragraph (a carriage return) is visible on screen like this: <
- When you print out a document, the line length on the paper is taken from the right margin setting and any left margin set within the Portfolio's Setup facility (see chapter 9).

THE WORD WRAP COMMAND

The Editor allows you to type continuously, and arranges the words for you on the screen. This is because the Editor automatically **word-wraps** the text. If a word will not fit on the current line, it is moved down to the next line and so on.

When the Editor command menu is displayed, the current word wrap state is shown alongside the **Word Wrap** command. To change the state (On to Off or vice versa), just select the Word Wrap command in the usual way. You are returned to the document with the word wrap state changed.

When word wrap is Off, you must press [Return] to end each line at a suitable point.

Remember that when word wrap in on, the end of each paragraph (a carriage return) is visible on screen like this: <.

THE MODE COMMAND

When typing text into the Editor, there are two basic typing modes, Insert and Overwrite. As the names suggest, Overwrite does just that and overwrites any existing text at the current cursor position. Insert mode inserts the newly typed text at the current cursor position, pushing the rest of the line across to the right.

The current mode is shown on the bottom right of the screen frame. If you have removed the screen frame with [F5], to check the mode, either press [F5] again to return the frame, or hold down the [Lock] key briefly - this calls back the information normally built into the bottom line of the screen frame. When you release [Lock] the information is removed.

To change modes, either hold down the [Shift] key and press [Del/Ins], or use the **Mode** command in the Editor command menu.

When the Editor command menu is displayed, the current typing mode is displayed alongside the **Mode** command. To change the command (Insert to Overwrite or vice versa) just select the **Mode** command in the usual way. You are immediately returned to your document with the new mode in effect.

THE HELP COMMAND

The Portfolio has two built-in help systems. The first is accessible when using the application programs - just press [F2]. This system gives help on the keyboard, clipboard, undeleting and the function keys.

The second help system is available from the main command menu in each of the application programs, where the last command is **Help**.

When you select **Help** from the Editor main command menu, the screen shows:

```
══════ Help ══════
Menus
File handling
```

The first menu option gives help on the Editor command menu and its sub-menus. The second option gives specific help on the use of the **Files** commands, concerned with loading and saving files.

In each of the help options, the help is in the form of a text file which you can read through by pressing the [↑] and [↓] keys. To return from one of the help files to the **Help** menu, press [Esc].

9

SETUP

The Portfolio's Setup facility in the application menu is a tool which allows you to customise the way the Portfolio works. Setup has sections on the display, the applications, sound, printing, the optional RS-232 connector and a built-in set of file transfer programs.

THE SETUP COMMANDS

When you select Setup from the Portfolio application menu, the screen shows:

```
 Setup 40556
Display...
Sounds...
Applications...
Printer...
RS-232 port
File transfer...
```

CONTROLLING THE DISPLAY

The **Display** command in Setup allows you to set the Portfolio's display mode according to the type of software in use. When you select Display from the Setup menu, the screen shows:

```
═══════ Display ═══════
External Mode...   Normal
Internal Mode...   Normal
Refresh...         Normal
Speed...           Normal
```

External & Internal Modes

The **External Mode** command is used to select the display mode when running external software, for example, from a memory card. The three display modes are **Normal**, **Static** and **Tracked**. The **Internal Mode** command sets the display mode used by DOS. The settings for Internal Mode and External Mode may be different. The three display modes operate as follows:

Normal	The normal 40 by 8 Portfolio display is used
Static	The full 80 by 25 pc display is used. You can move a 40 by 8 'window' around this larger screen (see below)
Tracked	The full 80 by 25 pc display is used. The 40 by 8 window is automatically moved around the 80 by 25 screen to 'track' the cursor.

In Internal Mode, the 40 by 8 window can be moved by the following keys:

[Alt] + a cursor key	Move one column or one line

[Fn] [Alt] + a cursor key	Move 20 columns or 6 lines.

When you exit from an external program, if the **External Mode** setting is different to the **Internal Mode** setting, the message **Press any key to continue** is displayed on the screen. This is to allow you to read any information displayed by the external program after you exit the program. Use the [Alt] key and the cursor keys as described above, to read this information.

If you only use the Portfolio's built in programs, i.e. DOS and the applications, you should leave both the Internal Mode and External Mode settings on Normal.

The Refresh Command

The Portfolio has an area of memory dedicated to the screen display - *display memory*. Some external programs display information by placing characters in this area of memory. The text only becomes visible when the Portfolio 'refreshes' the display from display memory.

The **Refresh** command allows you to select the way in which the display is refreshed. When you select **Refresh** from the **Display** menu, the following choices are offered:

Normal	No refresh is performed from the display memory; the Portfolio assumes you are only using the built-in applications which print information directly to the screen, by-passing display memory
Timed	The display is refreshed from display memory at the interval set using the **Speed** command described below
Keys	The display is refreshed from display memory whenever the current program waits for a keypress, but not during processing (for example, when the

Worksheet is recalculating). This is the recommended setting when running external programs

Both The display is refreshed from display memory at the interval set using the **Speed** command below **and** whenever the current program waits for a keypress.

The Speed Command

When using **Timed** or **Both** refresh modes, the display may be refreshed at one of two intervals; **Normal** (every 128 seconds) or **Fast** (every second).

Unless your software really requires a frequent screen refresh, it is recommended that you use **Normal**. Using **Fast** speeds up the rate at which the display is refreshed, but consumes a great deal more processor time, so slowing down the speed at which the Portfolio works.

CONTROLLING SOUND

The **Sounds** command in the Setup menu is used to control the Portfolio's use of sound. When you select **Sounds** from the Setup menu, the screen shows:

```
        Sounds
 Key Click     On
 Alarms        On
 Buzzer        On
 Mute Toggle
```

The first three commands in the menu show alongside the current settings of the named sounds. The default setting of all of these commands is On.

The Key Click Command

The **Key Click** command is used to switch on or off the Portfolio's key click.

The Alarms Command

The **Alarms** command is used to switch on or off the sound made by Diary alarms. When this command has been used to switch off alarms, any Diary alarms which become due are still displayed on the screen, but no audible alarm is sounded.

The Buzzer Command

At certain times, for example, when an error message is displayed, the Portfolio sounds a buzzer. This command may be used to silence this buzzer.

The Mute Toggle Command

The three commands above may each be set independently, but the **Mute Toggle** command allows you to set all three on or off together. This is useful if you are going into a meeting where you don't want any sound from the Portfolio to disturb proceedings.

If any of the above settings are On, when you select the **Mute Toggle** command all are set to Off. Select **Mute Toggle** again and all three are set to On.

THE APPLICATIONS COMMAND

The **Applications** command in the Setup menu, as the name suggests, is used to control a number of features of the Portfolio's built-in application programs.

When you select **Applications** from the Setup menu, the screen shows:

```
Applications
Clipboard save  On
Undelete save   On
Language
Keyboard
```

The Clipboard save Command

When you use the clipboard in the applications, as described in chapter 3, any information placed in the clipboard is temporarily stored in a file called **clipbord.dat** in the directory **\system**.

When you then leave the applications and return to DOS, there are two possibilities; either the file **clipbord.dat** is saved for later use or it is deleted. The **Clipboard save** command is used to select one of these options.

When the **Applications** menu is displayed, the current **Clipboard save** setting is shown alongside the command. To change the setting, just select the command in the usual way. The setting shown on the screen is changed from On to Off or vice versa.

The Undelete save Command

When you use the [F4] key in the applications to delete information, as described in chapter 3, all deleted information is temporarily stored in a file called **undelete.dat** in the directory **\system**.

When you then leave the applications and return to DOS, there are two possibilities; either the file **undelete.dat** is saved for later use or it is deleted. The **Undelete save** command is used to select one of these options.

When the **Applications** menu is displayed, the current **Undelete save** setting is shown alongside the command. To change the setting, just select the command in the usual way. The setting shown on the screen is changed from On to Off or vice versa.

The Language Command

When you first use the Portfolio you are offered the choice of three languages, English, French or German. The **Language** command allows you to change the Portfolio's operating language from that first chosen.

When you select **Language** from the **Applications** menu, the screen offers the three same languages; press [E] for English, [F] for Français or [D] for Deutsch.

The application programs operate entirely in the chosen language. For example, in the Worksheet, files saved in any language will, when loaded, be displayed with the functions shown in the current language.

DOS always requires you to type in commands in their English form, but the response may include text in the currently selected language.

The Keyboard Command

Having chosen your language with the **Language** command above, you may want to change the keyboard into that used in the corresponding country. In Britain the QWERTY layout is used; in France AZERTY and in Germany QWERTZ.

Select the layout by pressing [E] for English, [F] for Français or [D] for Deutsch. The keyboard then operates according to the chosen layout. Remember though that the legends on the keytops will not change, so the key pressed may give some other character than the one printed upon it.

PREPARING TO PRINT

To attach the Portfolio to any type of printer, you will need the following:

For a Serial Printer	Portfolio RS-232 adapter; a crossed serial cable (D type, 9 pin female to D type, 25 pin male)
For a Parallel Printer	Portfolio parallel adapter; a Centronics printer cable.

Having connected your Portfolio to the printer via a serial or parallel cable as appropriate, you need to make a number of printer settings via the **Printer** command in the Setup menu.

THE PRINTER COMMAND

When you select the **Printer** command from the Setup menu, the screen shows:

```
════════ Printer ════════
Destination      Parallel
Lines per page         66
Setup code
End of line...
Margins...
```

Printer: Destination

The **Printer** command allows you to set the destination of your printed output. The command offers three options, **Parallel**, **Serial** and **File**. You can select either **Parallel** or **Serial** according to the type of printer you have, or select **File**. The current **Printer** setting is shown in the menu alongside the command.

The **File** option allows you to specify a file name, to which all printed output will be directed. So, for example, you might specify the file name **print.out**. When you then use the **Print** command in any of the applications, the output will be sent to a file. If the file already exists, the printed information is added to the end of the file. If the file does not already exist, the file is created and the printed information written to it.

If you do not specify a file extension, the print file is given the extension **.prn**.

Printer: Lines per page

Different paper sizes can accommodate different numbers of lines of text. At a line spacing of 6 lines per inch, Letter size paper (8.5" x 11") is 66 lines long, while A4 size paper (210mm x 297mm) is 70 lines long. The **Lines per page** option allows you to set the number of lines of text to be printer per page. Valid page lengths are 0 or 41 to 99 lines. If you set the page length to 0 lines, no page breaks are inserted into the print stream, the text is printed as one continuous document.

Printer: Setup code

Some printers might require a setup string of commands before use, to enable some features of the printer, or select a particular print style. The **Setup** option allows you to enter a setup string for your printer.

When you select **Setup code** from the Printer menu, the screen shows:

```
Setup Code
Send:
```

You can now type in any setup code required by your printer. For example, the Epson FX-80 printer can print in double-strike mode. The command to initialise this print mode is ESC G (ASCII 27 followed by upper case G). If the characters in your setup string are typeable, then they can be typed directly. Otherwise you can enter them as three digit ASCII codes, or a mixture of the two.

Using the example above of ESC G, you would type:

```
027G [Return]
```

When you press [Return] you are returned to the **Printer** menu. The setup code typed now appears alongside the command in the menu. Now whenever a file is printed, the setup string is sent to the printer before any text.

Printer: End of line

Some printers require a carriage return and a line feed at the end of a line, others need only a carriage return. The **End of line** option has three settings:

CR	A single carriage return
CR-LF	A carriage return/line feed pair
CR-LF-LF	A carriage return followed by two line feeds.

Try printing on your printer with the default setting, **CR-LF**. If the printer prints correctly, leave the setting as it is. If the text all prints on one line, change the setting to **CR-LF-LF**. If the text prints double spaced, change the setting to **CR**.

On printers which need a carriage return line pair, the **CR-LF-LF** setting can be used to double space all text, but remember to halve the number of lines per page (see the **Lines per page** option above).

Printer: Margins

When the Portfolio prints out your files, it takes its margin settings from the **Margins** option in the **Printer** menu.

When you select **Margins**, the screen shows the current settings for the top, left and bottom margins. The default settings are:

Left	8
Top	6
Bottom	2.

Each of the margins may be set to any value in the range 0 to 20 lines or characters.

THE RS-232 PORT

The **RS-232 Port** option in the Setup menu allows you to set the data transfer speed (Baud rate), the parity and the number of data and stop bits used in communications via the optional RS-232 adapter.

Chapter 14 describes in some detail the way computers communicate via RS-232 ports. You should read that chapter if you are at all unsure about what the RS-232 is all about.

The default settings of the communications parameters (shown in bold type) and the other possible settings are shown below:

Baud Rate	**9600**, 4800, 2400, 1200, 600, 300, 150, 110
Parity	**None**, Even, Odd
Data Bits	**7**, 8
Stop Bits	**1**, 2

The final option in the **RS-232 Port** menu is **Initialize!**. After you have changed the settings for the above parameters, select **Initialize** to fix the new settings in memory. **If you do not select Initialize, the correct settings will not be in force when you need to use the RS-232 port.**

Make sure the RS-232 adapter is connected to your Portfolio before selecting **Initialize** or an error message will be displayed.

FILE TRANSFER

The optional parallel communications adapter allows you to print from the Portfolio to any parallel printer. It also allows you to transfer files between the Portfolio and a desk-top pc. The parallel adapter comes with full instructions for use. You should not attempt to use any of the facilities in the **File Transfer** menu without first fitting the parallel communications adapter and reading the manual supplied with that product.

10

THE WORKSHEET

THE BASICS

The Portfolio Worksheet is a spreadsheet program. A spreadsheet is like a sheet of paper ruled with horizontal and vertical lines. The lines form boxes. In the spreadsheet, each box is called a *cell*.

A CELL

A cell can be used to hold a number, some text or a formula. A column of cells can be used to store a series of figures; then a cell somewhere else on the grid can be used to store the total of that column of figures. But you don't have to add the figures up, the spreadsheet does it for you.

There are other things too that the spreadsheet can do for you. Every cell in the grid can act like a very powerful calculator. You just need to decide how to arrange your basic figures, and the spreadsheet calculates everything you need to know.

THE FIRST SCREEN

So let us take a look at the Portfolio Worksheet. When you select the Worksheet from the main applications menu, the screen shows:

```
┌ C:UNNAMED.WKS ══════════════════════════╗
│A1:                                      ║
│  ┌─────A────┼────B────┼────C────┼────D──║
│1 │                                      ║
│2 │                                      ║
│3 │                                      ║
│4 │                                      ║
└ Thu 09 Aug 90 10:30 ════════════════════╝
```

CELL REFERENCES

You can see just the top left corner of the grid of cells. The columns are lettered A, B, C and so on (across 127 columns; A to DW) and the rows are numbered 1 to 255. Cells are referred to by their column and row, so the top left cell is A1, the cell to its right is B1 and the cell below is A2. A cell name made up from one or two letters and a number is called a *cell reference*. The letters in a cell reference may be typed in upper or lower case.

CELL RANGES

Later on we will look in detail at how cells can be referred to in groups, known as cell *ranges*. For now though, you need only know that to refer to a rectangular block of cells, you specify the top left cell and the bottom right cell, separated by two dots. So to refer to the four cells A1, B1, A2 and B2, you would use the *range reference* A1..B2. A range reference may refer to any rectangular block of cells up to the size of the whole grid.

MOVING AROUND THE GRID

Initially, the *cursor*, a flashing block, is in cell A1. The cursor shows the *current cell*. Try moving around the grid by pressing the cursor keys at the bottom right of the keyboard. The [←] and [→] keys take you one cell in either direction. The [↑] and [↓] keys take you one cell up or down. It couldn't be simpler.

When you have a large number of cells in use, you may find moving one cell at a time is a little tedious, so there are a number of other key presses which take you around the grid more quickly. These are listed below:

Key Press	**Action**
[→]	move one cell right
[←]	move one cell left
[↑]	move one cell up
[↓]	move one cell down
[Home]	move to cell A1
[Tab]	move one screen right
[Shift] [Tab]	move one screen left
[Pg Up]	move 2/3 of one screen up
[Ctrl] [Pg Up]	move to row 1 in the current column
[Pg Dn]	move 2/3 of one screen down
[Ctrl] [Pg Dn]	move to last used row in current column.

ENTERING INFORMATION

Entering information in any cell is very straightforward. Just move to any cell in the grid and type a number. For example, move to cell B2. The screen shows:

```
╓ C:UNNAMED.WKS ══════════════════════════╗
B2:                                       ║
     ┌──────A────┼────B────┼────C────┼────D─║
1    │                                    ║
2    │                                    ║
3    │                                    ║
4    │                                    ║
╙ Thu 09 Aug 90 10:30 ════════════════════╝
```

Notice that the cell reference of the current cell is always shown at the top left of the screen.

Now type a number. For example, type:

```
260858 [Return]
```

Always press the [Return] key after entering information into a cell. The screen now shows:

```
╓ C:UNNAMED.WKS ══════════════════════ ≈ ╗
B2: 260858                               ║
     ┌──────A────┼────B────┼────C────┼────D─║
1    │                                    ║
2    │             260858                 ║
3    │                                    ║
4    │                                    ║
╙ Thu 09 Aug 90 10:30 ════════════════════╝
```

The number appears in the cell, the cursor still flashes on the same cell and the top left of the screen shows the current cell reference and the contents of the current cell. Note also the 'changed' symbol at the top right corner of the screen border.

Now let us enter some text. Press the move to cell C2. Type:

```
This is text [Return]
```

The screen now shows:

```
╓ C:UNNAMED.WKS ══════════════════════ ≈ ╗
C2: 'This is text                        ║
     ┌──────A────┼────B────┼────C────┼────D─║
1    │                                    ║
2    │             260858 This is text    ║
3    │                                    ║
4    │                                    ║
╙ Thu 09 Aug 90 10:30 ════════════════════╝
```

The text appears in the current cell, and notice that it overlaps into the next cell as it is too long to fit inside the cell width of 9 characters. We can change the cell width, but this will come later.

Notice also that the text is automatically aligned at the left of the cell. This can be changed too; text can be aligned left, right or centre. This is described in detail below.

Now let us enter a *formula*. A formula can be entered into any cell. A formula may be as simple as a straightforward addition of two numbers, or it may be a complex formula made up of mathematical functions and references to other cells in the grid. These are some examples of formulae:

+100+200	adds two numbers
+B2	takes value from cell B2
+B2+500	takes value from cell B2 and adds 500
+B2*2	takes value from cell B2 times 2
+B2/4.3	takes value from cell B2 over 4.3
@SQRT(B2)	square root of value from cell B2
@LN(B2)	log of value from cell B2
@LN(B2)+ @SQRT(2)	log of value from cell B2 plus the square root of 2
@PI	Constant Pi (3.14159...)
@SUM(B3..D9)	adds values of cells in range B3 to D9

Every cell can be used in this way as a powerful calculator. You can perform arithmetic on numbers, include the values from other cells into calculations and use any of a wide range of mathematical functions and constants.

So let's type in these example formulae. The ones which call on the value of the cell B2 assume you have typed in the number 260858 as described above. Go to the following cells and type the formulae as shown below:

Go to Cell	Type	Displayed Value
B3	+100+200	300
B4	+B2	260858
B5	+B2+500	261358
B6	+B2*2	521716
B7	+B2/4.3	60664.65
B8	@SQRT(B2)	510.7426
B9	@LOG(B2)	5.416404
B10	@LOG(B2)*@SQRT(2)	7.659952
B11	@PI	3.141593
B12	@SUM(B3..B5)	522516

Parentheses (this type of brackets) may also be freely used. For example +(1+2)/(2+3) gives the result 0.6. You can also use a range of *functions* such as PI, SUM and LOG, all of which are preceded by the character @. These are described in chapter 11.

THE DISPLAY VALUE

When you have typed a number or a formula into a cell, the way it is displayed on the screen may vary according to the settings made for the current cell; the numeric format, the number of decimal places, whether a currency character is used and so on. The contents of a cell is the information which you typed in. The *display value* is the way the contents are displayed by the Worksheet.

DATA DEFINITIONS

When you type information into a cell and press [Return], the Worksheet interprets it as text, a number or a formula as follows:

Numbers & Formulae

If information typed into a cell starts with any of these characters:

`+ - 0 1 2 3 4 5 6 7 8 9 ( @ #`

or a decimal point, the Worksheet interprets it as a number or a formula.

The following table shows, in order of precedence, the operators which may be used in formulae:

^	powers
+ -	unary plus, unary minus
* /	multiply, divide
> < = <= >= <>	relationals
#NOT#	logical NOT
#AND#, #OR#	logical AND, logical OR

A formula may be up to 240 characters long when typed in.

Text

If information typed into a cell starts with any character other than those shown under the heading Numbers & Formulae above, it is interpreted as text. In particular, there are four characters which have special meanings:

’	Normal left aligned text
^	Centre aligned text
“	Right aligned text

\ Duplicates the text across the width of the cell.

The last of these , \, can be used to provide a horizontal divider or highlight. For example, type:

```
\=- [Return]
```

in any cell in a standard 9 character wide column and the cell will show:

```
=-=-=-=-=
```

This could be used as an underline or separator between one area of the grid and another.

A piece of text typed into one cell may be up to 240 characters long.

Deleting Information

To delete the contents of any cell, move the cursor to that cell and press the [Del] key. To delete the contents of more than one cell at a time, use the **Range: Erase** command described in chapter 11.

Changing Information

To change the contents of any cell, move the cursor to that cell and press [Return]. The contents of the cell is placed on the top line of the screen, just as if you had only just typed it in. You can now use the cursor keys to move to any part of the cell contents, change the information and again press [Return].

CELL REFERENCES

Cell references, as described earlier in this chapter, consist of one or two letters to designate a column and a number to designate a row. These two parts specify one particular cell in the grid. However, when typing a cell reference as part of a formula, there are three forms the cell reference may take; *relative*, *absolute* or *mixed*. These different types of cell reference are described fully in chapter 11 under the heading The Range: Copy Command.

RANGE PAINTING

When typing in a formula, there is an easy way to call on the value of a particular cell, or block of cells, as part of that formula. The cell or cells are 'painted' over by moving the cursor. This process is called *range painting*.

Let us return to the examples we typed in earlier in this chapter. The numbers and formulae we typed in are as follows:

Cell	**Formula**	**Displayed Value**
B3	+100+200	300
B4	+B2	260858
B5	+B2+500	261358
B6	+B2*2	521716
B7	+B2/4.3	60664.65
B8	@SQRT(B2)	510.7426
B9	@LOG(B2)	5.416404
B10	@LOG(B2)*@SQRT(2)	7.659952
B11	@PI	3.141593
B12	@SUM(B3..B5)	522516

Move to cell B8 and press the [Del] key. The formula in that cell will be deleted. Now we will type in the same formula using range painting to select cell B2 as part of the formula.

Type the first part of the formula just as you did before:

`@SQRT(` but do not press [Return]

Now press the [↑] key. The screen changes to show a double-lined box around the cell above B8. The screen border is now a single-lined box. The screen will show something like this:

```
C:UNNAMED.WKS                          ≈
B7: @SQRT(B7
        A     |     B     |     C     |     D
5
6
7
8
Thu 09 Aug 90 10:30
```

Now you can move the box around by just pressing the cursor keys.

As you move the box, note that the current cell indicator on the top line changes to show the new position of the box. The formula you have started is also visible, but as you move the box around, the cell reference in the formula is changed to that of the cell highlighted by the box. Move the box around the grid a little and watch how the formula changes.

Now move the box up to cell B2 and finish the formula by typing the closing bracket. You are returned to cell B8; the formula is shown on the top line beside the cell reference and the result is displayed in the cell.

You might have wanted to enter another cell reference as part of the formula, for example:

```
@SQRT(B3+B3)
```

In which case, after specifying cell B2 by range painting, you would type the '+' and then use the cursor keys again to range paint the second cell.

To paint a whole range of cells, a similar method can be used. For example, you might want to select a rectangular block of cells between B3 at the top left and D10 at the bottom right, as part of the formula:

```
@SUM(B3..D10)
```

Type in the first part of the formula:

```
@SUM(
```

and press one of the cursor keys. Move the cursor up to the first cell in the range - B3. Press the [.] key. This fixes the top left corner of the range. Now, as you move around, you will see that the box expands, the current cell marking the bottom right corner of a rectangular block of cells.

The formula on the top line will show:

```
@SUM(B3..C3
```

with the final cell reference showing the current position in the grid. Move around again and see this reference change. Now move to the bottom right cell of the required range, D10, and type the closing bracket. The formula will now read @SUM(B3..D10).

The process of range painting is also used in some of the Worksheet commands, described in chapter 11.

CIRCULAR REFERENCES

It is possible, when typing in a formula, to make the result from the formula dependent upon the formula itself. For example, in an example earlier in this chapter, we entered:

Cell	Formula	Displayed Value
B4	+B2	260858

If we had typed into cell B4, the formula +B4, the formula would be attempting to read its own value for display in the cell B4. The resulting display value is 0.

This phenomenon, where a the value of a cell is dependent upon itself, is called a *circular reference.* When a circular reference appears anywhere in the grid, a small circle is displayed just below the current cell reference at the top left of the screen.

A circular reference may be more convoluted than this simple example. For example, a cell might contain a formula which calls the value of another cell elsewhere on the grid. So far so good, but that second cell might already call on the value of the first cell. Again we have a circular reference.

In very specialised cases a circular reference may be just what you need. However, usually you will find that if the circle symbol appears on your screen, you may want to look carefully at the layout of your information.

THE [End] KEY

There is one more way of moving rapidly around the grid which was not mentioned earlier; that is by using the [End] key followed by a cursor key or the [Home] key.

When you press the [End] key followed by the [↑] or [↓] key, the cursor moves up or down until it reaches the first or last cell in a group of cells in the current column. Similarly, when you press the [End] key followed by the [←] or [→] key, the cursor moves left or right until it reaches the first or last cell in a group of cells in the current row. If there are no more used cells in the current row or column in the chosen direction, the cursor stops at the edge of the grid.

When you press the [End] key followed by the [Home] key, the cursor moves to the cell at the end of the currently used area in the grid. This cell may be empty, but if a range of cells was selected with A1 at the top left and this cell at the bottom right, every used cell in the grid would fall within that range.

When the [End] key has been pressed, a small arrow appears under the current cell reference at the top left corner of the screen. If you press [End] and wish to cancel it, without moving from the current cell, just press [End] again.

PLANNING A WORKSHEET FILE

When planning your sheet, a little forethought can make the job a great deal easier later on. Most sheets have the following features:

- Raw data
- Sub-totals
- Results
- Other Information.

The Raw data is made up from the numbers which the Worksheet is crunching for you. The Sub-totals might be interim figures based on your raw data. The Results are the final figures the sheet is designed to produce. Under the catch-all title of Other Information might come your text headings, perhaps an explanatory note on one or more cells and any text used as dividers or underlines (e.g. =-=-).

There is no fixed way in which you should arrange the parts of your sheet, we all like to work in the way that suits us best. However, the following points might be useful:

- A neat sheet is easier to read and probably better organised than one which looks messy
- Use concise, but readable, column and row headings
- A summary of the sheet's uses somewhere at the top left corner may be useful if you return to the sheet after a period away
- If your sheet produces results in just a few cells, group them together so they can all be seen on the screen together

- If your sheet uses the same constant in a number of formulae (the interest rate; the tax rate; a commodity price), put the figure in one cell and refer to that cell from all of your formulae. If the figure changes suddenly, you only have to change the figure in the one cell.

Finally, if the Worksheet produces results which you think are way out - check your figures, then check the path of logic from your raw data through one formula into another and eventually into your results. The error will probably jump out at you somewhere along the way.

11

WORKSHEET COMMANDS & FUNCTIONS

This chapter describes each of the Portfolio Worksheet commands and the full list of functions which are available. The next chapter gives gives some useful example sheets which employ some of the commands and functions described in this chapter.

THE WORKSHEET COMMAND MENU

To view the Worksheet command menu, press [F1]. The screen shows:

```
Grid 40800
Files...
Worksheet...
Range...
Goto
Defaults...
Help...
```

Note that, if you are used to using Lotus 1-2-3, with which the Portfolio Worksheet is file compatible, you can press [/] to call the same command menu.

The Worksheet commands are presented in the usual menu format. Some of the options in the menu lead to further menus and options. The full range of options and commands is described below.

THE FILES MENU

When you select **Files** from the Worksheet command menu, the screen shows:

```
Files
New
Load...
Save as...
Print
```

The use of the **Files** commands is very much the same in each of the file-based applications. A full description of using these commands can be found in chapter 3 under the heading THE FILES COMMANDS. This section gives a brief round-up of the description found there.

The Files: New Command

If you have made any changes to the current file since it was last saved, the file changed symbol will be shown at the upper right corner of the screen frame. If you then select the **Files: New** command, the Portfolio prompts you to save the file, complete with its changes. The screen shows:

```
Save Current?
Yes
No
```

Select **Yes** to save the file under the current file name (shown on the top line of the screen frame), or select **No** to discard the current file **including any changes you have made since the last time the file was saved**.

The Files: Load Command

The **Files: Load** command is used to load an existing file from a drive into an application. A copy of the file is made from the original which is stored on the drive - loading a file does not have any effect on the original file, unlike saving (see the **Files: Save as** command below).

When you select the **Files: Load** command, the Portfolio prompts you to enter the name of the file you want to load. The screen shows:

```
═══════════ Load ═══════════
Name: C:\SHEETS\UNNAMED.WKS
```

The default file name (shown in the dialogue box) is always the file name most recently used by the current application program. If the current file name is, for example, **unnamed.wks,** that is the file name offered by the dialogue box. You now have four options:

1. Press [Return] to load the file shown in the dialogue box

2. Edit the file name to that of the file you want to load

3. Press the [*] key to see all files from the current application

4. Press the [:] key to see a list of all of the files and sub-directories found in the current directory.

Note that item 3 in the list above is the equivalent to typing *.* (see chapter 4 for more details of this in relation to DOS). You can also type a new, full path name with or without a file name, including wildcards, just like those used in DOS.

Note that when you load a Worksheet file, any @Functions which appear in your formulae are automatically displayed in the current language (see chapter 9 on the Setup facility for details of changing language). So if you type in a formula such as:

```
@SUM(B1..D4)
```

Then save the sheet, change the Portfolio's operating language to French or German and return to the same sheet, the formula would now read as one of the following:

`@SOMME(B1..D4)`	French
`@SUMME(B1..D4)`	German.

The Files: Save as Command

The **Files: Save as** command is used to save a copy of the current file under the same or a different name on any drive. If there is already a copy of the file under the name you use, **the old copy will be overwritten by the new copy**, so make sure you are not losing some vital information by using an existing file name.

If you save a new copy of a file under a name different from that of the original file, then the original file will be unaffected when you make your new copy.

For further details of the way in which file names are given, refer to the section above under the heading The Files: Load Command.

Note: The Golden Rule when using any type of computer is this - and there are no exceptions:

Always make a back-up copy of any file which is really important.

You can make a copy onto a memory card or via the optional communications link to a desk-top pc. Then if disaster strikes, you still have a copy of your important data.

The Files: Print Command

The **Print** command is used to print the contents of the current file to a printer (serial or parallel) or to a file on a drive. For more information on the destination of your printed output, see the section under the heading PREPARING TO PRINT in chapter 9.

When the **Files: Print** command is selected, the screen shows:

```
 ====== Print ======
 Range       A1..H52
 Width            70
 Go!
```

The three options in the **Files: Print** menu are described below; the process is as follows:

- Select a **Range** of cells to be printed, from a single cell to the whole of the grid
- Select a **Width**, according to the width of the paper in your printer as a number of characters
- Select **Go!** to send the output to the printer (or file).

Note that the destination of the printed output, the page length, margins and so on must be set from within the Setup facility. See chapter 9 for further details of Setup.

The Print: Range Command

The **Print: Range** command is used to set the range of cells to be printed, but does not itself send any output to the printer - see the **Go!** command below. The cell range shown in the menu is the extent of used cells in the current file, or, if **Print** has been used before with the current file, the range of cells last printed. If you are happy with the print range shown, select **Go!** (see below).

When you select the **Range** command, the display returns to the current file, showing a double-lined box around the current cell:

```
 C:UTILITY.WKS ────────────────── ≈
C2: +B2/(A2/4.546)
    ────A───┼───B───┼───C───┼───D──
1  │ Litres   Miles
2  │    29.2      248│38.60986│
3  │
4  │
 Thu 09 Aug 90 10:30 ─────────────
```

You may now:

- Press [Return] to start range-painting a range of cells using the current cell as the anchor. When you are happy with the print range shown, press [Return] and select **Go!** (see below)
- Press [Esc] to release the anchor cell, ready to move to another and continue range-painting as above
- Type a new cell range to be printed. The cell range should be typed in the format:

```
              A1..C2
Top left cell /    \ Bottom right cell
```

As soon as you start typing the new cell range, the double-lined box is removed from the screen and the new range is shown on the top line of the screen. When you have entered the new range, press [Return] and select **Go!** (see below).

The Print: Width Command

The **Print: Width** command allows you to set a width for the printed output, according to the width of the paper in your printer, as a number of characters. The allowed range is 2 to 240 characters. Most page sized printers will print 80 characters across, but remember to check any margin settings fixed from within the Setup facility (see chapter 9).

The Print: Go! Command

When you have selected a range of cells to be printed, set a width for the output and you are sure you are happy with the settings in the Setup facility, select **Go!** to print the information.

THE WORKSHEET MENU

When you select **Worksheet** from the main Worksheet command menu, the screen shows:

```
 Worksheet
Recalc     On
Titles     Off
Insert...
Delete...
Window...
Erase
```

The options in the **Worksheet** menu allow you to set automatic or manual recalculation of the grid; use a part of the grid for titles which are then always visible; insert or delete a number of rows or columns; flip between two windows on the grid and erase the whole contents of the grid.

The Worksheet: Recalc Command

When you start entering text, numbers and formulae into the grid, every time you press [Return] to complete a new cell entry, the grid is recalculated. Of course, when there are only a few cells in use, this process is instantaneous. Later on, you may find that in a large sheet using many complex formulae, when you press [Return] at the end of a cell entry, or you press [F9] to recalculate the grid, the recalculating process takes a little longer.

The **Recalc** command allows you to turn off the Worksheet's automatic recalculation. Then when you are entering a large number of complex formulae, the grid is not automatically recalculated every time you put a number or a formula in a cell.

When you look at the **Worksheet** menu, the current recalculation mode is shown at the right of the menu. In the case of the menu shown above, automatic recalculation is on. Select **Recalc** to turn automatic recalculation off.

Remember that when you have finished entering your data, you can either stay with manual recalculation, pressing [F9] when you want the grid to be recalculated, or you can select **Recalc** again from the **Worksheet** menu to return to automatic recalculation.

The Worksheet: Titles Command

When you have built up a large sheet containing information spread over many rows and column of the grid, you may need to regularly refer to information in the top one or two rows or leftmost one or two columns of the grid. For example, you have a sheet which you are using to find which supplier of car parts gives the cheapest overall price for a number of different parts. The sheet looks like this:

	A	B	C	D	E	F
1	KIT-CAR COSTING CHART					
2						
3	Part Name	Qty	Partfinder		Kit-Shop	
4			Each	Tot.	Each	Tot.
5						
6	Engine block	1	$237.00	$237.00	$403.00	$403.00
7	Cylinder head	1	$110.00	$110.00	$155.00	$155.00
8	Manifold	2	$40.00	$80.00	$72.00	$144.00
9	Pistons	12	$33.50	$402.00	$30.00	$360.00
10	Piston rings	24	$1.00	$24.00	$2.25	$54.00
12	Exhaust pipe	2	$48.00	$96.00	$61.00	$122.00
13	Transmission	1	$199.00	$199.00	$185.00	$185.00
14	Gearbox	1	$554.00	$554.00	$448.00	$448.00
15	Steering	1	$125.00	$125.00	$125.00	$125.00
16	Wheels	5	$95.00	$475.00	$103.50	$517.50
17	Fenders	2	$55.60	$111.20	$41.02	$82.04
18	Chassis	1	$950.00	$950.00	$722.00	$722.00
19	Body shell	1	$1,099.00	$1,099.00	$660.00	$660.00
20						
21	Total Kit Prices>>>			$4,462.20		$3,977.54

As you move the cursor around the grid, the column of Part Names at the left of the grid is no longer visible. The **Worksheet: Titles** command is used to make one or more rows and columns into *titles* which are then always displayed on the screen, regardless of the position of the cursor on the grid.

The rule to remember is that, when you set Titles On, all cells currently visible above and to the left of the current cell will be fixed on the screen until you set Titles Off.

In the example above, to keep the leftmost column and the top four rows constantly displayed, you should move the cursor to cell B5 (just below and to the right of the rows and columns you want to use as titles), then select the **Titles** command from the **Worksheet** menu. Now when you move the cursor around the grid, the part names and shop names are always visible.

For example, if you had set the titles as described above, pressed [F5] to remove the screen frame and then moved the cursor to cell E16, the screen would show:

```
E16: (C2) [W10] 55.6
        A          D          E
3  | Part Name             Partfinder
4  |             Tot.      Each
5  |
14 | Steering    $218.00   $125.00   >
15 | Wheels      $492.50    $95.00   >
16 | Fenders      $79.98    $55.60   >
```

Note that you can see column A, shown on the screen next to column D. Similarly, rows 3, 4 and 5 are shown next to rows 14, 15 and 16. The information in the grid has not been rearranged, it is just displayed in such a way as to make the best use of the large grid.

Note also that the top line of the screen shows that the current cell is E16, and is set to Currency format at 2 decimal places, with a cell width of 10 characters; the value in the cell is 55.6.

When titles have been set, you cannot move the cursor into the area used as titles. To edit any cell in that area, use the **Goto** command to move the cursor to the required cell. See the description of the **Goto** command later in this chapter.

At the end of the session with the current sheet, whether or not you save the sheet after setting Titles On, the titles setting is discarded. You may also switch off the use of titles by selecting the command again from the **Worksheet** menu.

The Worksheet: Insert Command

When you are building a Worksheet file, the best way is to plan the sheet before you start. Decide where your main numeric entry cells will be; where your results will be displayed and any particular features which you will need to refer to most often. See the end of chapter 10 for some hints on designing your Worksheet file.

However, you may one day need another column or another row **in between** the rows and columns of figures and formulae you have already typed in. The Portfolio

Worksheet allows you insert one or more rows or columns just where they are needed. (You can delete rows and columns too - see the **Delete** command below.)

Inserting Rows

To insert one or more rows, first position the cursor anywhere on the row you would like to be pushed down by the newly inserted rows. For example, if you want to insert two new rows of cells between rows 2 and 3, first move the cursor to any cell in row 3. Select **Insert** from the **Worksheet** menu. The screen shows:

```
Insert
Row
Col
```

Select **Row** and the screen shows the current cell in a double lined box. You can now range-paint the number of rows you want to insert. When the required number of rows are shown in the box, in this case two, press [Return]. The rows below the cursor are pushed down by the required number and you now have your new, blank rows.

Inserting Columns

To insert one or more columns, first position the cursor anywhere in the column you would like to be pushed across by the newly inserted columns. For example, if you want to insert two new columns of cells between columns B and C, first move the cursor to any cell in column C. Select **Insert** from the **Worksheet** menu. The screen shows:

```
Insert
Row
Col
```

Select **Col** and the screen shows the current cell in a double lined box. You can now range-paint the number of columns you want to insert. When the required number of columns are shown in the box, in this case two, press [Return]. The columns to the right of the cursor are pushed to the right by the required number and you now have your new, blank columns.

Cell References

It doesn't matter if some of your formulae refer to cells on the other side of the insertion. When the new rows or columns are put in place, any cell references in formulae anywhere in the grid which might be affected by the new rows or columns are automatically adjusted by the Worksheet.

At The Edge

There is one thing to remember when inserting rows or columns; do not try to insert so many rows or columns that any existing data is pushed off the right or bottom edge of the grid. If you attempt to do so, the Worksheet will respond with the message **Too Many Cols or Rows** and no insertion will be made.

The Worksheet: Delete Command

When you are building a Worksheet file, the best way is to plan the sheet before you start. Decide where your main numeric entry cells will be; where your results will be displayed and any particular features which you will need to refer to most often.

However, you may one day decide you no longer need any of the information in one or more whole rows or columns. The Portfolio Worksheet allows you to delete any number of rows or columns, causing all other cells to the right or below the deleted cells to move back to fill the gap. (You can insert rows and columns too - see the **Insert** command above.)

Deleting Rows

To delete one or more rows, first position the cursor anywhere on the first row you would like to delete. For example, if you want to delete the whole of rows 3 and 4, first move the cursor to any cell in row 3. Select **Delete** from the **Worksheet** menu. The screen shows:

```
Delete
Row
Col
```

Select **Row** and the screen shows the current cell in a double lined box. You can now range-paint the rows you want to delete. When the required number of rows are shown in the box, press [Return]. The rows in the box are then all deleted. All rows below are moved up to fill the gap.

Deleting Columns

To delete one or more columns, first position the cursor anywhere in the leftmost column you would like to delete. For example, if you want to delete the whole of columns B and C, first move the cursor to any cell in column B. Select **Delete** from the Worksheet menu. The screen shows:

```
Delete
Row
Col
```

Select **Col** and the screen shows the current cell in a double lined box. You can now range-paint the number of columns you want to delete. When the required number of columns are shown in the box, in this case two, press [Return]. The columns in the box are then deleted. All columns to the right then move across to the left to fill the gap.

Cell References

If some of your formulae explicitly refer to cells in the rows and columns which are deleted, those formulae will be changed to include ERR (error) in place of the cell reference. This is to bring to your notice the fact that a previously correct formula now attempts to refer to cells which have been deleted.

If, on the other hand, one of your formulae refers to a block of cells, **from within which** one or more rows or columns have been deleted, the formula is automatically adjusted by the Worksheet to take account of the now smaller range of cells.

For example, in this small sheet, cell B1 contains the formula @SUM(A1..A3), which adds the values of the three cells A1, A2 and A3:

```
 C:EXAMPLE.WKS
B1: @SUM(A1..A3)
   ------A-----+-----B-----+-----C-----+-----D--
1  |        10         60
2  |        20
3  |        30
4  |
 Thu 09 Aug 90 10:30
```

If you delete row 2 by using the **Delete** command as described above, the formula in cell B1 is changed to read @SUM(A1..A2) and the screen shows:

```
 C:EXAMPLE.WKS
B1: @SUM(A1..A2)
   ------A-----+-----B-----+-----C-----+-----D--
1  |        10         40
2  |        30
3  |
4  |
 Thu 09 Aug 90 10:30
```

When you delete any rows or column from your sheet, ALWAYS take care that the results of your formulae are still in line with your original plans. If in doubt, check!

The Worksheet: Window Command

When you have built a sheet covering a large area of the grid, it is sometimes a little awkward having to move from one area, say the place where you insert your critical figures, to the place where the results appear. The **Worksheet: Window** command allows you to easily flip between two cells anywhere on the sheet.

To mark any cell as the one you want to quickly return to, select the **Window** command from the Worksheet menu. The screen shows:

```
Window
Mark
Flip (F10)
```

Select **Mark**. Now when you move the cursor around the grid, you can return to the marked cell by either selecting **Flip** as above or by just pressing [F10]. Wherever you move on the grid and whatever cells are visible, you can always return to the marked cell with a single keypress.

If you press [F10] again without first moving the cursor, the cursor returns to the place from which it jumped to your marked cell.

If you press [F10] without first having marked a cell, the cursor always returns to cell A1.

The Worksheet: Erase Command

The **Worksheet: Erase** command is used to erase the contents of the whole grid. If you have changed any part of the sheet since it was last saved, when you select **Erase** the screen shows:

```
Are You Sure?
Yes
No
```

If you select **No**, you are returned to your intact sheet. If you select **Yes**, the information in all cells is discarded, all column widths are reset to 9 characters, the numeric display format is set to General (see the **Range: Format** and **Defaults: Format** commands later in this chapter), the default text alignment is set to Left (see the **Defaults: Text align** command) and the Window Mark is set to cell A1.

THE RANGE MENU

The **Range** menu contains commands which operate on just a specified range of cells in the grid, rather than the whole grid. To effect changes on the whole grid, see the section later in this chapter under the heading THE DEFAULTS MENU.

The Range: Copy Command

Usually a sheet is built up from a number of repeating features. You might have a list of figures in one column and, alongside them, a series of formulae which calculate some result from the raw figures.

For example, in the sheet we used earlier in this chapter, column A contains a list of car parts; column B contains the required quantity of each part; columns C and D and also E and F contain the cost of each part and a total of the part cost multiplied by the part quantity.

There are only a dozen or so parts in our example sheet, so the number of formulae to be typed is small, but in a real-life situation there might be one or two hundred. The **Range: Copy** command allows you to enter your formula in one cell and then copy that cell, or a range of cells, to a much bigger range of cells.

The process is as follows:

- Move the cursor to the top left cell in the range to be copied - the **source range**
- Select the **Range: Copy** command
- Range-paint the source range
- Press [Return]
- Move the cursor to the top left cell in the **destination range**
- Press [Return].

Here is our example sheet, with the car parts and quantities in place, but not the prices or formulae:

```
      A            B     C         D         E       F
1  KIT-CAR COSTING CHART
2
3  Part Name      Qty   Partfinder          KitShop
4                       Each      Tot.      Each    Tot.
5
6  Engine block     1
7  Cylinder head    1
8  Manifold         2
9  Pistons         12
10 Piston rings    24
12 Exhaust pipe     2
13 Transmission     1
14 Gearbox          1
15 Steering         1
16 Wheels           5
17 Fenders          2
18 Chassis          1
19 Body shell       1
20
21 Total Kit Prices>>>
```

The next step is to put into cell D6 the formula:

```
+$B6*C6
```

Now, until a number is entered into cell C6, the display value of the formula is 0.

This formula can now be copied to all of the cells in the range C7..C19. Move the cursor to cell C6 and select the **Range: Copy** command. The current cell is shown in a double-lined box. As we are only copying a single cell, press [Return] to select that cell as the source range (C6..C6).

Press the [↓] key once to move the cursor down to the start of the destination range and press [Return]. The formula from C6 is then copied into every cell in the destination range.

You can now copy that column of formulae into column E under the name of the second parts shop. This time, the source range is C6 to C19 and the destination range is E6 to E19.

Absolute & Relative Cell References

Here we should take a look at the formula we copied and the ones which appear in the destination ranges, because they differ slightly.

As was mentioned briefly in chapter 10, there are two basic types of cell reference; *absolute* and *relative*. There are also *mixed* cell references, which we will come to in a moment.

An absolute cell reference refers to a particular cell in the grid, for example, the reference A1 refers to the cell in row 1 and column A of the grid - the top leftmost cell. The $ signs in the reference indicate that the reference is absolute.

If you copy a formula containing an absolute cell reference to a cell somewhere else in the grid, the cell reference in the formula, A1, will always be the same and will always refer to the top leftmost cell in the grid.

A relative cell reference indicates a cell whose position in the grid is only given **relative** to the cell where the reference appears. For example, cell B1 might contain the formula:

```
+A1
```

So the display value of cell B1 is taken directly from cell A1 which is on the same row and one cell to the left. If the formula in cell B1 is now copied to cell D2, after copying, the formula in cell D2 is :

```
+C2
```

This is a different formula to the one copied, but it still refers to the cell on the same row and one cell to the left of the cell containing the formula.

Mixed Cell References

An absolute cell reference uses $ signs to indicate that the column and row are absolute positions in the grid; a relative cell reference uses none, and indicates a cell relative to the cell containing the reference. A **mixed cell reference** uses just one $ sign on either the row or the column.

For example, cell B1 might contain the formula:

```
+$A1
```

So the display value of cell B1 is taken directly from the cell one to the left, in column A. If the formula in cell B1 is now copied to cell D2, after copying, the formula in cell D2 is :

```
+$A2
```

This is a different formula to the one copied, but it still refers to the cell in column A and on the same row as the cell containing the formula.

The Range: Erase Command

To delete the contents of a single cell, just position the cursor on that cell and press [Del/Ins]. Obviously, to clear a whole range of cells in this way would be rather tedious, so instead we use the **Range: Erase** command.

To erase the contents of a range of cells, first position the cursor on the top left corner of the range or cells, then select the **Range: Erase** command. The current cell is then shown in a double-lined box. You can now range-paint the cells to be erased. When the required cells are all enclosed by the box, press [Return]. Any text, numbers or formulae in the selected range are all erased.

The Erase command does not affect any text alignment, numeric format or other settings on the cell, just the contents typed or copied into the cell.

The Range: Width Command

As you build a worksheet file, it is likely that you will want to change the width of some of the columns in the grid, so the cells are big enough to comfortably contain your data. To do this you use the **Range: Width** command.

If you type some text into a cell, and the text is longer than the width of the cell, the text spills out onto the next cell. However, if you type some information into the next cell, that information may overlap the text in the first cell. Also, if you type a long number into a cell, and there is not enough room for the Worksheet to display the number correctly, the cell just displays asterisks (***). In either of these cases you will want to make the columns a little wider.

To change the width of one or more columns, move the cursor to either the first (leftmost) or last (rightmost) column to be changed, then select the **Range: Width** command.

The screen shows:

```
==== Width ====
Width of Col:  9
```

You can now type in a column width of between 1 and 34 characters, and press [Return]. The screen then changes to show the current cell in a double-lined box. You can now range-paint the number of columns to be changed. When the correct number of columns is shown, press [Return].

It doesn't matter if the cells already contain information, only the width of the cells is changed - everything else remains the same.

You can change the default column width for the whole grid by using the **Defaults: Width of Col** command described later in this chapter.

The Range: Format Command

The Worksheet's primary function is to crunch numbers quickly and efficiently. It must then be able to display the results of its calculations in a suitable format. The Worksheet allows you to see your results in a whole variety of formats; to a fixed number of decimal places, in currency format with up to three currency characters, in scientific or engineering formats, in percent format or in general format.

You can use the **Range: Format** command to set the numeric format for just a range of cells, or the **Defaults: Format** command to set the numeric format for the whole grid.

When you select the **Range: Format** command, the screen shows a menu of the numeric formats available. The default numeric format on all cells is general format. That means that the Worksheet will attempt to display the number in the most economic manner it can.

The **Format** menu looks like this:

```
Format
Fixed
Scientific
Currency

General
Percent
```

Fixed Format

When displaying large amounts of numeric data, general format will make the numbers look uneven if they are all displayed to different numbers of decimal places. Using fixed format allows you to present the figures in a neat column, with all of the numbers being displayed to a set number of decimal places.

For example, here are three numbers as they would be displayed in general format and fixed format at 3 decimal places:

Cell Contents	General	Fixed
3.1415926535898	3.1415926535898	3.1416
27.98	27.98	27.9800
4	4	4.0000

Note that although the display value of the top number differs slightly from the actual cell contents, all calculations in the Worksheet are based on the true cell contents rather than the display value.

First move the cursor to the top left cell of the range to be changed. When you select **Fixed** from the Format menu, the screen shows:

```
Dec. places
0 to 12: 2
```

You can now type in the required number of decimal places between the limits shown. The screen changes to show the current cell in a double- lined box. You can now range-paint the cells where fixed format is to be used. When the correct range of columns is shown, press [Return].

It doesn't matter if the cells already contain information, only the numeric display format of the cells is changed - everything else remains the same.

You can change the default numeric format for the whole grid by using the **Defaults: Format** command described later in this chapter. See also Currency Format described below.

Scientific Format

Scientific format is commonly used for displaying very small or very large numbers in a small space. For example, here are three numbers as they would be displayed in full decimal format and scientific format at 3 decimal places:

Number	Scientific Format
0.0000000000268	2.680E-11
252500000	2.525E+08
3.1415926535898	3.142E+00

A number in scientific format consists of a number between 1 (inclusive) and 10 (exclusive), followed by a power. So in the second example above the scientific format number represents:

$$2.525 * 10^8$$

First move the cursor to the top left cell of the range to be changed. When you select **Scientific** from the Format menu, the screen shows:

```
Dec. places
0 to 12: 2
```

You can now type in the required number of decimal places between the limits shown. The screen then changes to show the current cell in a double-lined box. You can now range-paint the cells where scientific format is to be used. When the correct range of columns is shown, press [Return].

It doesn't matter if the cells already contain information, only the numeric display format of the cells is changed - everything else remains the same.

You can change the default numeric format for the whole grid by using the **Defaults: Format** command described later in this chapter. See also Engineering Format described below.

Currency Format

For sheets which contain large amounts of financial data, it is useful to be able to display the data using an appropriate currency format. The Portfolio Worksheet allows you to use any three characters as currency characters. For example, $, US$, £ or ¥.

The currency characters are set using the **Defaults: Format: Currency** command described later in this chapter. However, the **Range: Format: Currency** command is used to enable the use of currency format in a range of cells.

First move the cursor to the top left cell of the range to be changed. When you select **Currency** from the Format menu, the screen shows:

```
Dec. places
0 to 12: 2
```

You can now type in the required number of decimal places between the limits shown. The screen then changes to show the current cell in a double-lined box. You can now range-paint the cells where currency format is to be used. When the correct range of columns is shown, press [Return].

It doesn't matter if the cells already contain information, only the numeric display format of the cells is changed - everything else remains the same. The currency characters are part of the display format of the cell only, they are not added to the data itself.

You can change the default numeric format for the whole grid by using the **Defaults: Format** command described later in this chapter.

Decimal Point (,) Format

Some countries use the dot (.) character as a decimal point, others use a comma (,). Where the dot is used as the decimal point, a comma is used as the separator between blocks of three digits (the *triad separator*) and vice versa.

For example, in the USA and the UK, the decimal point is a dot, so we represent one million, in figures, as:

```
1,000,000.00
```

Here the triad separator has been used before every third digit shown before the decimal point. In some European countries, the dot and comma change places, so the same figure would be given as:

```
1.000.000,00
```

The **Range: Format: ,** command allows you to use triad separators in a range of cells. The particular separator in use (, or .) is set using the **Defaults: Decimal Point** command described later in this chapter. Note that the triad separator is only used before the decimal point.

First move the cursor to the top left cell of the range to be changed. When you select **,** from the Format menu, the screen shows:

```
Dec. places
0 to 12: 2
```

You can now type in the required number of decimal places between the limits shown. The screen then changes to show the current cell in a double-lined box. You can now range-paint the cells where the triad separator is to be used. When the correct range of columns is shown, press [Return].

It doesn't matter if the cells already contain information, only the numeric display format of the cells is changed - everything else remains the same. The triad separators are part of the display format of the cell only, they are not added to the data itself.

General Format

The default numeric format on all cells is general format. That means that the Worksheet will attempt to display the number in the most economic manner it can. If the whole number cannot be displayed in a cell, the number is displayed in scientific format (see above). If there is not enough room for the number to be displayed in scientific format (at least 5 characters), the cell displays asterisks (***). Use the **Range: Width** command to make the column wider so that the number can be displayed correctly.

General format can be reselected for ranges of cells which have previously been set to use one of the other formats.

Percent Format

The Worksheet displays percentages as decimal fractions. For example, if the interest rate for a particular period is 10%, you should enter 0.10 to represent that interest rate.

Percent format can be used to display percentages in their usual form, including the % sign. For example, the interest rate of 10% mentioned above, when entered as 0.10, is displayed in general format as **0.1**. When that cell is set to display percent format at 2 decimal places, it displays the figure as **10.00%**.

First move the cursor to the top left cell of the range to be changed. When you select **Percent** from the Format menu, the screen shows:

```
Dec. places
0 to 12: 2
```

You can now type in the required number of decimal places between the limits shown. The screen then changes to show the current cell in a double-lined box. You can now range-paint the cells where percent format is to be used. When the correct range of columns is shown, press [Return].

It doesn't matter if the cells already contain information, only the numeric display format of the cells is changed - everything else remains the same.

But Which Format?

When you have used the **Format** command to set the numeric format on a number of cells, the format of the cell is shown on the top line of the screen. For example, when the current cell is A1, the column width is 10 characters, the numeric format is currency and the cell contains the number 10, the top of the screen shows:

```
 C:EXAMPLE.WKS
A1: (C2) [W10] 10
          A          B          C          D
1        $10.00
2
3
```

The numeric format of the current cell is shown after the current cell reference at the top left of the screen as follows:

Format	Indicator	
Fixed	(F2)	at 2 decimal places
Scientific	(S2)	at 2 decimal places
Currency	(C2)	at 2 decimal places
,	(,2)	at 2 decimal places
General	(G)	
Percent	(P2)	at 2 decimal places

THE GOTO COMMAND

In chapter 10 a number of keyboard shortcuts are listed. These enable you to move the cursor rapidly to any place in the grid. Another tool which makes that process easier is the **Goto** command. **Goto** allows you to move immediately to any cell in the grid, including cells in an area set aside for titles (see the **Worksheet: Titles** command earlier in this chapter).

When the **Goto** command is selected the screen shows:

```
╔══ Goto ═══╗
║ Cell:     ║
╚═══════════╝
```

You can now type in the reference of any cell in the grid (A1 to DW255). When you press [Return], the cursor is immediately moved to the specified cell.

Note that if you use the **Goto** command to move the cursor to a cell in an area set aside for titles, you are able to move the cursor around the titles area in the usual way. However, if you then move out of the titles area, you will be unable to move back in - except by using the **Goto** command again.

THE DEFAULTS MENU

The commands in the **Format** menu, described earlier in this chapter, are used to set various features of selected cells in the grid. For example, the **Range: Format: Width** command is used to set the width of a selected number of columns.

The commands in the **Defaults** menu are used to set various features of **all** cells in the grid - the default settings.

When **Defaults** is selected, the screen shows:

```
═══ Defaults ═══
Decimal Point      .
Text Align      Left
Width of Col       9
Autoload         Yes
Format             G
Currency           $
```

The menu shows, alongside the commands themselves, the current default settings for all cells in the grid. The default settings and other options are:

Setting	**Default**	**Other options**
Decimal Point	. (dot)	, (comma)
Text Alignment	Left	Right, Centre
Column Width	9	
Autoload	Yes	No
Format	General	Fixed, Scientific, Currency, (comma), Percent
Currency	$	Any three characters

The Defaults: Decimal Point Command

As we saw earlier in this chapter in the section on the **Range: Format** command, some countries use the dot (.) character as a decimal point, other use a comma (,). Where the dot is used as the decimal point, a comma is used as the separator between blocks of three digits (**the triad separator**) and vice versa (see the **Range: Format** command above).

For example, in the USA and the UK, the decimal point is a dot, so we represent one and a half, in figures, as:

```
1.5
```

Which is exactly how the number should be typed. In some european countries, a comma is used as the decimal point, so the same number would be given as:

```
1,5
```

And again, this is exactly how the number should be typed. The **Defaults: Decimal Point** command allows you to set the default decimal point character for all the cells in the grid and therefore governs how numbers should be typed.

When the **Defaults** menu is displayed, the current decimal point character is shown in the menu. To change to the other decimal point character, just select the **Decimal Point** command in the usual way.

You should remember that if you select the comma as the decimal point character, you must then type numbers using the comma as the decimal point. If you then try to type a number using the dot as the decimal point, the Worksheet will report a **Syntax Error**.

When you change from one decimal point character to the other, it doesn't matter if the cells already contain information, only the numeric display format of the cells is changed - everything else remains the same. Commas in the display are converted into dots and vice versa.

The Defaults: Text Align Command

When using text in the Worksheet, you can choose to align the text to the left, right or the centre of the cell. The setting made with the **Defaults: Text Align** command is then used for the whole grid. You cannot, for example, select left aligned text as the grid default and then select right aligned text for just a range of cells.

When the **Defaults** menu is displayed, the current text alignment setting is shown in the menu:

```
Text Align
Left
Right
Centre
```

Select one of the alignment settings as required. Any cells which contain text are then displayed with the text aligned accordingly. When you change from one alignment to another, it doesn't matter if the cells already contain information, only the display format of the cells is changed - everything else remains the same.

The Defaults: Width of Col Command

As you build a worksheet file, it is likely that you will want to change the width of some of the columns in the grid, so the cells are big enough to comfortably contain your data. To do this you use the **Range: Width** command. However, to change the default column width for the whole grid, you use the **Defaults: Width of Col** command.

It is sometimes useful to have the leftmost column in the grid (column A) set wide enough to contain text titles, perhaps 16 characters wide, with the rest of the columns set rather narrower, perhaps 6 characters wide, to contain numeric data. In this case you would set the default column width to 6 characters with the **Defaults: Width of Col** command and then set the width of column A with the **Range: Width** command.

To change the default column width, select the **Defaults: Width of Col** command. The screen shows:

```
Width
Width of Col:  9
```

You can now type in a column width in the range 1 and 34 characters, then press [Return]. You are then returned to the grid, now with all columns displayed at the selected width.

It doesn't matter if the cells already contain information, only the width of the cells is changed - everything else remains the same.

The Defaults: Autoload Command

When you start the Worksheet, the most recently used Worksheet file is automatically loaded into memory when **Autoload** is enabled.

This feature allows you to return to the same file without having to use the **Load** command each time. If you are likely to use a different file each time you use the Worksheet, it might be better to switch autoloading off.

When the **Defaults** menu is displayed, the current autoload setting is shown in the menu. When you select **Autoload** from the **Defaults** menu, the setting is immediately toggled from Yes to No, or vice versa and you are returned to the grid.

The Defaults: Format Command

Earlier in this chapter we looked at the **Range: Format** command, which is used to set the numeric format for a range of cells in the grid. The **Defaults: Format** command works in the same way, but on the whole of the grid, rather than just a range of cells.

When you select the **Defaults: Format** command, the screen shows a menu of the numeric formats available. The default numeric format for the whole grid is general format. That means that the Worksheet will attempt to display the number in the most economic manner it can.

The **Defaults: Format** menu looks like this:

```
Format
Fixed
Scientific
Currency
,
General
Percent
```

Fixed Format

When displaying large amounts of numeric data, general format will make the numbers look uneven if they are all displayed to different numbers of decimal places. Using fixed format allows you to present the figures in a neat column, with all of the numbers being displayed to a set number of decimal places.

For example, here are three numbers as they would be displayed in general format and fixed format at 4 decimal places:

Cell Contents	General	Fixed
3.1415926535898	3.1415926535898	3.1416
27.98	27.98	27.9800
4	4	4.0000

Note that although the fixed format display value of the top number differs slightly from the actual cell contents, all calculations in the Worksheet are based on the true cell contents rather than the display value.

When you select **Fixed** from the **Format** menu, the screen shows:

```
Dec. places
0 to 12: 2
```

You can now type in the required number of decimal places between the limits shown. When you press [Return] the display returns to the grid with the new setting in force.

It doesn't matter if the cells already contain information, only the numeric display format of the cells is changed - everything else remains the same.

Scientific Format

Scientific format is commonly used for displaying very small or very large numbers in a small space. For example, here are three numbers as they would be displayed in full decimal format and scientific format at 3 decimal places:

Number	**Scientific Format**
0.0000000000268	2.680E-11
252500000	2.525E+08
3.1415926535898	3.142E+00

A number in scientific format consists of a number between 1 (inclusive) and 10 (exclusive), followed by a power. So in the second example above the scientific format number represents:

$$2.525 * 10^{8}$$

When you select Scientific from the Format menu, the screen shows:

```
Dec. places
0 to 12: 2
```

You can now type in the required number of decimal places between the limits shown. When you press [Return], the display returns to the grid with the new setting in force.

It doesn't matter if the cells already contain information, only the numeric display format of the cells is changed - everything else remains the same.

Currency Format

For sheets which contain large amounts of financial data, it is useful to be able to display the data using an appropriate currency format. The Portfolio Worksheet allows you to use any three characters as currency characters. For example, $, US$, £ or ¥.

The currency characters are set using the **Defaults: Currency** command described later in this chapter. However, the **Defaults: Format: Currency** command is used to enable the use of currency format in all cells in the grid.

When you select **Currency** from the **Format** menu, the screen shows:

```
Dec. places
0 to 12: 2
```

You can now type in the required number of decimal places between the limits shown. When you press [Return], the display returns to the grid with the new setting in force.

It doesn't matter if the cells already contain information, only the numeric display format of the cells is changed - everything else remains the same. The currency characters are part of the display format of the cell only, they are not added to the data itself.

Decimal Point (,) Format

Some countries use the dot (.) character as a decimal point, others use a comma (,). Where the dot is used as the decimal point, a comma is used as the separator between blocks of three digits (**the triad separator**) and vice versa.

For example, in the USA and the UK, the decimal point is a dot, so we represent one million, in figures, as:

```
1,000,000.00
```

Here the triad separator has been used before every third digit shown before the decimal point. In some european countries, the dot and comma change places, so the same figure would be given as:

```
1.000.000,00
```

The **Defaults: Format: ,** command allows you to use triad separators in all cells in the grid. The particular separator in use (, or .) is set using the **Defaults: Decimal Point** command described earlier in this chapter. Note that the triad separator is only used before the decimal point.

When you select , from the **Format** menu, the screen shows:

```
Dec. places
0 to 12: 2
```

You can now type in the required number of decimal places between the limits shown. When you press [Return], the display returns to the grid with the new setting in force.

It doesn't matter if the cells already contain information, only the numeric display format of the cells is changed - everything else remains the same. The triad separators are part of the display format of the cell only, they are not added to the data itself.

General Format

The default numeric format on all cells is general format. That means that the Worksheet will attempt to display the number in the most economic manner it can. If the whole number cannot be displayed in a cell, the number is displayed in scientific format (see above). If there is not enough room for the number to be displayed in scientific format (at least 5 characters), the cell displays asterisks (***). Use the **Range: Width** or **Defaults: Width of Col** command to make the column wider so that the number can be displayed correctly.

Percent Format

The Worksheet displays percentages as decimal fractions. For example, if the interest rate for a particular period is 10%, you should enter 0.10 to represent that interest rate.

Percent format can be used to display percentages in their usual form, including the % sign. For example, the interest rate of 10% mentioned above, when entered as 0.10, is displayed in general format as **0.1**. When that cell is set to display percent format at 2 decimal places, it displays the figure as **10.00%**.

When you select **Percent** from the **Defaults: Format** menu, the screen shows:

```
Dec. places
0 to 12: 2
```

You can now type in the required number of decimal places between the limits shown. When you press [Return], the display returns to the grid with the new setting in force.

It doesn't matter if the cells already contain information, only the numeric display format of the cells is changed - everything else remains the same.

The Defaults: Currency Command

When your sheet contains a large amount of financial data, it is useful to display the figures with an appropriate currency indicator. The Portfolio Worksheet allows you use any three characters as currency indicators. Here are just a few which you might want to use:

US$	United States Dollars
HK$	Hong Kong Dollars
DM	Deutschmarks
Yen	Japanese Yen

When you select the **Currency** command from the **Defaults** menu, the screen shows:

```
= Currency =
Symbol(s): £
```

The default currency character, shown on the screen, is the pound character £. You can now type any three characters to use as a currency indicator, then press [Return]. The display returns to the grid. Any cells which use currency format are shown using the currency indicators just typed.

Note that, in addition to the characters you can type on the keyboard in the usual way, there are other characters in the Portfolio's *character set*. These are all shown in the ASCII table in appendix A.

For example, in the last of the four examples shown above, the word Yen is given in full. There is, however, a Yen sign, (¥), in the Portfolio's character set, at character 157. This character can be used for display purposes on the Portfolio but cannot be printed on some printers. If your printer uses the standard IBM compatible character set, then the Yen symbol can be printed, otherwise use Yen in full.

THE HELP COMMAND

The Portfolio has two built-in help systems. The first is accessible when using the application programs - just press [F2] (hold down [Fn] and press [2]). This system gives help on the keyboard, clipboard, undeleting and the function keys.

The second help system is available from the main command menu in each of the application programs, where the last command is **Help**.

When you select Help from the Worksheet's main command menu, the screen shows:

```
═══ Help ═══
Worksheet Menus
File handling
@Functions
```

The first menu option gives help on the Worksheet command menu and its sub-menus. The second option gives specific help on the use of the Files commands, concerned with loading and saving files. The last option gives help on the Worksheet's @Functions - so called because they all start with the character @. These are described in some detail in the following section.

In each of the three help options, the help is in the form of a text file which you can read through by pressing the [↑] and [↓] keys. To return from one of the help files to the **Help** menu, press [Esc].

THE WORKSHEET @FUNCTIONS

@ABS(exp)

The @ABS function returns the absolute, or positive, value of the argument **exp**.

For example:

```
@ABS(-24)
```

will return 24, the absolute value of -24.

The absolute value of a positive number is also positive, so:

```
@ABS(26)
```

will return 26.

See also @ROUND.

@ACOS(exp)

The @ACOS function returns the angle that has a cosine of **exp**. The angle returned is in radians.

See also @ASIN, @ATAN, @ATAN2, @COS, @SIN, @TAN.

@ASIN(exp)

The @ASIN function returns the angle that has a sine of **exp**. The angle returned is in radians.

See also @ACOS, @ATAN, @ATAN2, @COS, @SIN, @TAN.

@ATAN(exp)

The @ATAN function returns the angle that has a tangent of **exp**. The angle returned is in radians.

See also @ACOS, @ASIN, @ATAN2, @COS, @SIN, @TAN.

@ATAN2(exp1,exp2)

The @ATAN2 function returns the angle that has a tangent of **exp1/exp2**. The function uses the signs of **exp1** and **exp2** to return a value in the correct quadrant. The value is returned in radians.

See also @ACOS, @ASIN, @ATAN, @COS, @SIN, @TAN.

@AVG(list)

The @AVG function returns the arithmetic mean (average) of the values expressed in the argument **list**. For example:

```
@AVG(26,31,35,40,41,42)
```

will return the result 35.83333, the average of the values given in the list.

If **list** contains any blank cells, they will be ignored by the @AVG function. For this reason, ensure that all zero values in your sheet are entered as 0 and not left as blank cells. For example, based on this sheet:

```
        A      B
  1
  2    31
  3    35
  4    40
  5    41
  6    42
  7
```

The formula:

```
@AVG(A1..A6)
```

will return a value of 37.8, having calculated the average of values contained in the five cells, A2 to A6. If, however, 0 is entered into cell A1:

```
        A      B      C
  1     0
  2    31
  3    35
  4    40
  5    41
  6    42
  7
```

The formula:

```
@AVG(A1..A6)
```

will return a value of 31.5, the average of values in all six cells from A1 to A6.

See also @COUNT, @MAX, @MIN, @STD, @SUM, @VAR.

@CHOOSE(exp,list)

This function returns the item at position **exp** in **list** where the first item in the list is at position 0. The values in list cannot be expressed as a cell range and must, therefore be entered into the formula. For example, assuming that cell D14 contains the value 5:

```
@CHOOSE(D14,42,41,40,35,31,26)
```

will return 26, the item at position 5 in the list (the sixth item).

See also @HLOOKUP, @VLOOKUP.

@COS(exp)

The @COS function returns the cosine of the angle **exp**. The argument **exp** must be in radians.

See also @ACOS, @ASIN, @ATAN, @ATAN2, @SIN, @TAN.

@COUNT(list)

The @COUNT function returns the number of non-blank cells in **list**. Cell ranges may be included in list. If zero appears in any of the cells in **list** the @COUNT function evaluates the cell as non-blank and it is, therefore, counted. For example:

```
        A      B
1      45
2       1
3       0
4       5
5      25
6     213
7
8      59
9
```

The formula:

```
@COUNT(A1..A8)
```

will return a value of 7, indicating that there are seven non-blank cells in the given range.

See also @AVG, @MAX, @MIN, @STD, @SUM, @VAR.

@DATE(year,month,day)

The @DATE function returns the number of days between 30 December 1899 and the date given by the arguments **year**, **month** and **day**. For example:

```
@DATE(1990,8,18)
```

will give the value 33103 because there are 33103 days between 30 December 1899 and 18 August 1990.

One use of this function is to calculate the number of days between a set starting date and the current date. You may, for example, want to know the days elapsed since the start of the financial year. Assuming the current date is 18 August 1990, the formula:

```
@TODAY-@DATE(90,4,1)
```

gives the result 139, showing that 139 days have passed since the financial year began.

See also @DAY, @MONTH, @TODAY, @YEAR.

@DAY(exp)

Using the @DAY function it is possible to extract the day of the month from the argument **exp**, where **exp** is the number of days elapsed since 30 December 1899. For example:

```
@DAY(33103)
```

will return 18, showing that 33103 days after 30 December 1899 will be on the 18th day of the month in which it falls.

See also @DATE, @MONTH, @TODAY, @YEAR.

@ERR

This function can be used to report the occurrence of any condition which you deem to be an error. For example:

```
@IF(M15<10,@ERR,M15*.0135)
```

The @IF function checks the contents of cell M15 and reports an error if it finds a value lower that 10. If not, the contents of M15 will be multiplied by .0135.

See also @ISERR.

@EXP(exp)

This function returns the arithmetic constant **e** (2.71828...), raised to the power of the argument **exp**. For example:

```
@EXP(12)
```

will return a value of 162755.

@FALSE

This function returns a value of 0.0. For example, cell N74 could contain 1 to indicate the occurrence of a certain condition. So, the formula:

```
@IF(N74=@FALSE,B74,A74)
```

would return the contents of A74 because the contents of N74 (1) do not equal @FALSE (0.0). If N74 did contain 0.0, the above formula would return the contents of B74.

See also @IF, @TRUE.

@FV(pmnt,int,term)

The @FV function is used to calculate the future value of a regular, fixed investment given the arguments **pmnt** (the regular investment), **int** (the fixed rate of interest) and **term** (the term over which the investment is made).

Suppose you decide to invest $1,000 per year for the next 35 years and your bank offers you a fixed interest rate of 12.5%. To calculate the future value of your investment, the @FV function is used as follows:

```
@FV(1000,0.125,35)
```

giving the result 485660.3793.... or $485,660.38 (the numeric format of the cell containing this formula can be set, as described earlier in this chapter, to display the result as currency).

The rate of interest (**int**) must be given as a decimal, so the rate of 12.5% appears in the example as 0.125.

See also @IRR, @NPV, @PMT, @PV.

@HLOOKUP(exp,range,idx)

The @HLOOKUP function performs a horizontal lookup on the range of cells specified by **range**. The first row in the range contains a number of comparison values. These values must be in increasing order and there must be no duplicates. The function finds the last cell in this row that has a value of less than or equal to **exp** and returns the value contained in the cell which is **idx** rows below. Non-integer values of **exp** are truncated to their integral part.

For example, based on this worksheet the results below would be produced:

	A	B	C	D	E	F
1	1	2	3	4	5	
2	12	14	17	20	27	
3	14	16	21	23	30	
4	17	20	25	29	34	
5	21	27	32	39	41	
6						

Formula	**Result**
@HLOOKUP(1,A1..E5,1)	12
@HLOOKUP(3,A1..E5,4)	32
@HLOOKUP(5,A1..E5,2)	30
@HLOOKUP(2,A1..E5,7)	ERR

In the last example, the function returned ERR because **idx** specified a cell below the given range. This also happens if **idx** is given as a negative value or is equal to the number of rows in **range**. If **idx** is given as zero, the function returns the value of the cell at the top of the column, i.e. the comparison value itself.

See also @CHOOSE, @VLOOKUP.

@IF(exp,then,else)

If the @IF function finds that the condition **exp** returns TRUE (1.0), the value of **then** is returned. If the condition **exp** returns FALSE (0.0), the value of **else** is returned. For example, assuming that cell J18 contains 26:

```
@IF(J18<25,150,50)
```

will return 50 because the content of cell J18 (26) is greater than 25.

See also @FALSE, @TRUE.

@INT(exp)

The @INT function returns the integer or whole number part of **exp**.

For example:

```
@INT(14.2)
```

will return the value 14, ie, only that part of **exp** which appears before the decimal point.

@IRR(exp,range)

This function is used to calculate the approximate internal rate of return from a series of discounted cash flow. In other words, it calculates the interest rate that would give a net present value of zero on the cash flows. The function requires two arguments; **exp**, which represents an initial guess at the likely interest rate and **range**, the list of positive and negative cash flows (incoming and outgoing). Cash flows are taken to occur at the start of each period. For example, the worksheet below represents an initial payment of $2,000 and five receipts of $575. The guess at the likely interest rate of interest (11.5%) is shown as a decimal in cell C6.

	A	B	C
1	-2000		
2	575		
3	575		
4	575		
5	575		
6	575		0.115
7			

The formula:

```
@IRR(C6,A1..A6)
```

would return a value of 0.13458 representing an internal rate of return of 13.458% on the initial investment.

See also @FV, @NPV, @PMT, @PV.

@ISERR(exp)

This function returns TRUE (1.0) if the argument **exp** returns ERR and otherwise returns FALSE (0.0). For example, assuming that cell A9 contains 0 and A10 contains 244/A9:

```
@ISERR(A10)
```

would return 1.0 because A10 contains an illegal divide by zero.

See also @ERR.

@ISNA(exp)

This function returns TRUE (1.0) if the argument **exp** returns NA and otherwise returns FALSE (0.0). For example, assuming that cell B57 contains @IF(B58=31,89,@NA):

```
@ISNA(B57)
```

would return TRUE if the content of B58 is not equal to 31 and would return FALSE if the content of B58 was equal to 31.

See also @NA.

@LN(exp)

This function returns the natural (base e) logarithm of the argument **exp**. For example:

```
@LN(589.3)
```

will return a value of 6.37894.

See also @LOG.

@LOG(exp)

This function returns the base 10 logarithm of the argument **exp**. For example:

```
@LOG(589.3)
```

will return a value of 2.77034.

See also @LN.

@MAX(list)

This function returns the highest value found in **list**. For example:

```
@MAX(26,41,42,35,40,31)
```

would return 42, the highest value.

Any text strings that occur in **list** are treated as zero.

See also @AVG, @COUNT, @MIN, @STD, @SUM, @VAR.

@MIN(list)

This function returns the lowest value found in **list**. For example:

```
@MIN(26,41,42,35,40,31)
```

would return 26, the lowest value.

Any text strings that occur in **list** are treated as zero.

See also @AVG, @COUNT, @MAX, @STD, @SUM, @VAR.

@MOD(exp1,exp2)

This function returns the remainder when **exp1** is divided by **exp2** (modulo). For example:

```
@MOD(26,6)
```

will return a value of 2.

@MONTH(exp)

Using the @MONTH function it is possible to extract the month from the argument **exp**, where **exp** is the number of days elapsed since 30 December 1899. For example:

```
@MONTH(33103)
```

will return 8, showing that 33103 days after 30 December 1899 will be in the eighth month of the year in which it falls.

See also @DATE, @DAY, @TODAY, @YEAR.

@NA

This function returns NA (Not Available). For example:

```
@IF(B58=31,89,@NA)
```

if the content of cell B58 is equal to 31, a value of 89 is returned, otherwise, NA is returned.

See also @IF, @ISNA.

@NPV(int,range)

This function returns the Net Present Value of a series of discounted cash flows for a given rate of interest per period. The **range** of values contains the positive and negative cash flows (incoming and outgoing), and **int** (the rate of interest) must be expressed as a decimal. The cash flows are taken to occur at the end of each period. For example, the worksheet below represents an initial payment of $2,000 and five receipts of $575. The rate of interest is 11.5% (shown as a decimal in cell C6).

```
        A        B        C
  1     -2000
  2     575
  3     575
  4     575
  5     575
  6     575               0.115
  7
```

The formula:

```
@NPV(C6,A1..A6)
```

would return a net present value of 88.502, representing a return of $88.50 on the investment. The numeric format of the cell containing this formula can be set, as described earlier in this chapter, to display the result as currency.

See also @FV, @IRR, @PMT, @PV.

@PI

This function returns the value of the mathematical constant Pi (3.142...).

@PMT(prin,int,term)

The @PMT function is used to calculate a loan payment, given the arguments **prin** (the sum borrowed), **int** (rate of interest) and **term** (the term of repayment). For example, mortgage repayments can be calculated using the @PMT function.

Suppose a sum of $125,000 is to be borrowed at an annual interest rate of 13.5% and repaid over 25 years. To calculate the monthly repayment, the @PMT function is used as follows:

```
@PMT(125000,0.135/12,300)
```

giving the result 1457.056.... or $1,457.06 (the numeric format of the cell containing this formula can be set, as described earlier in this chapter, to display the result as currency).

In the example, the interest rate of 0.135 (13.5%) is divided by 12 to give the monthly rate of interest and 300 is the number of months in the 25 year repayment period.

See also @FV, @IRR, @NPV, @PV.

@PV(pmnt,int,term)

The @PV function is used to calculate the present value of an annuity given the arguments **pmnt** (the regular investment), **int** (the fixed rate of interest) and **term** (the term over which the investment is made).

For example, suppose you decide to invest $500 per year for the next 15 years and your bank offers you a fixed interest rate of 9%. To calculate the present value of your investment, the @PV function is used as follows:

```
@PV(500,0.09,15)
```

giving the result 4030.3442.... or $4,030.34 (the numeric format of the cell containing this formula can be set, as described earlier in this chapter, to display the result as currency).

The rate of interest (**int**) must be given as a decimal, so the rate of 12.5% appears in the example as 0.125.

See also @IRR, @NPV, @PMT.

@RAND

The @RAND function returns a random, floating point number within the range 0.0 (inclusive) to 1.0 (exclusive).

@ROUND(exp1,exp2)

The @ROUND function rounds **exp1** to the nearest division by 10 as specified by **exp2**. The argument **exp2** can be greater or less than 0. Where **exp2** is less than 0, **exp1** is rounded to the nearest 10^@ABS(exp2). This function can, therefore, round a number to the nearest million or to a number of decimal places.

The following list of examples shows the values returned when 3482178.6345695 (**exp1**) is rounded to a different values of **exp2**.

Formula	Result
@ROUND(3482178.6345695,-5)	3500000.00000
@ROUND(3482178.6345695,-3)	3482000.00000
@ROUND(3482178.6345695,-1)	3482180.00000
@ROUND(3482178.6345695,0)	3482179.00000
@ROUND(3482178.6345695,1)	3482178.60000
@ROUND(3482178.6345695,3)	3482178.63500
@ROUND(3482178.6345695,5)	3482178.63457

See also @ABS.

@SIN(exp)

The @SIN function returns the sine of the angle **exp**. The argument **exp** must be in radians.

See also @ACOS, @ASIN, @ATAN, @ATAN2, @COS, @TAN

@SQRT(exp)

The @SQRT function returns the square root of the argument **exp**. For example:

```
@SQRT(732)
```

will return the value 27.0555.

@STD(list)

This function returns the standard deviation of the values in **list**. For example, based on this worksheet:

```
        A       B
  1    25
  2    14
  3    19
  4    32
  5    12
  6    17
  7    22
  8    26
  9
```

The formula:

```
@STD(A1..A8)
```

would produce a result of 6.25375.

See also @AVG, @COUNT, @MAX, @MIN, @SUM, @VAR.

@SUM(list)

This function returns the sum of all the numbers in **list**. For example, based on this worksheet:

	A	B
1	45	
2	1	
3	0	
4	5	
5	25	
6	213	
7	14	
8	59	
9		

The formula:

```
@SUM(A1..A8)
```

would produce a result of 362.

Any text strings that occur in **list** are treated as zero.

See also @AVG, @COUNT, @MAX, @MIN, @STD, @VAR.

@TAN(exp)

The @TAN function returns the tangent of the angle **exp**. The argument **exp** must be in radians.

See also @ACOS, @ASIN, @ATAN2, @COS, @SIN.

@TODAY

The @TODAY function returns the number of days elapsed between 30 December 1899 and the current date. For example, assuming the current date is 18 August 1990, the @TODAY function will return the value 33103.

See also @DATE, @DAY, @MONTH, @YEAR.

@TRUE

This function returns a value of 1.0. For example, cell N74 could contain 0 to indicate the occurrence of a certain condition. So, the formula:

```
@IF(N74=@TRUE,B74,A74)
```

would return the contents of A74 because the contents of N74 (0) do not equal @TRUE (1.0). If N74 did contain 1.0 then the above formula would return the contents of B74.

See also @FALSE, @IF.

@VAR(list)

This function returns the statistical variance of the values in **list**.

See also @AVG, @COUNT, @MAX, @MIN, @STD, @SUM.

@VLOOKUP(exp,range,idx)

The @VLOOKUP function performs a vertical lookup on the range of cells specified by **range**. The first column in the range contains a number of comparison values. These values must be in increasing order and there must be no duplicates. The function finds the last cell in this column that has a value of less than or equal to **exp** and returns the value contained in the cell which is **idx** columns to the right. Non-integer values of **exp** are truncated to their integral part.

For example, based on this worksheet the results below would be produced:

	A	B	C	D	E	F
1	1	12	14	17	21	
2	2	14	16	20	27	
3	3	17	21	25	32	
4	4	20	23	29	39	
5	5	27	30	34	41	
6						

Formula	**Result**
@VLOOKUP(1,A1..E5,1)	12
@VLOOKUP(3,A1..E5,4)	32
@VLOOKUP(5,A1..E5,2)	30
@VLOOKUP(2,A1..E5,7)	ERR

The last example, the function returned ERR because **idx** specified a cell to the right of the given range. This also happens if **idx** is given as a negative value or is equal to the number of columns in **range**. If **idx** is given as zero, the function returns the value of the cell at the left of the row, ie the comparison value itself.

See also @CHOOSE, @HLOOKUP.

@YEAR(exp)

Using the @YEAR function it is possible to extract the year from the argument **exp**, where **exp** is the number of days elapsed since 30 December 1899. For example:

```
@YEAR(33103)
```

will return 90, showing that 33103 days after 30 December 1899 will fall during 1990.

See also @DATE, @DAY, @MONTH, @TODAY.

12

SOME WORKSHEET EXAMPLES

The examples we have seen in the previous chapters have been useful only for explaining various aspects of using the Portfolio Worksheet. Now let us look at some example sheets which you can really use.

All of these example sheets appear on a disk available from TTP, along with a suite of PostScript printing programs. See chapter 13 for details.

To clear any information you have typed into the Worksheet, press the following keys to use the Files: New command (this is described fully in chapter 11):

```
[F1] [F] [N] [N]
```

The whole grid will be cleared and you are ready to start entering new information.

A MILES-PER-GALLON CALCULATOR

You want to work out how many miles to the gallon your car is averaging, but the petrol pumps are marked only in litres. This is a (very) small sheet which works out your running average MPG.

For those who have never done this with a piece of paper and a pencil, this is how the calculation works. First fill your tank. Set your trip meter on the dashboard to zero or record the mileage on the mileometer. Drive until the tank is close to empty (not too close...) and then refill. Note the number of miles travelled since the last fill and the number of litres you put in the tank this time.

Now for the calculation. The following equation gives you the miles per gallon (there are 4.546 litres to one gallon):

$$\text{MPG} = \frac{\text{miles travelled}}{(\text{litres} / 4.546)}$$

Here is how the Worksheet can perform the calculation for you. Enter the following text and formulae into the cells shown, and press [RETURN] after each entry:

Go to Cell	**Type**
A1	^Litres
B1	^Miles
C1	^MPG
C2	+B2/(A2/4.546)

Note the use of the ^ character to centre the text in the cell.

The screen will show:

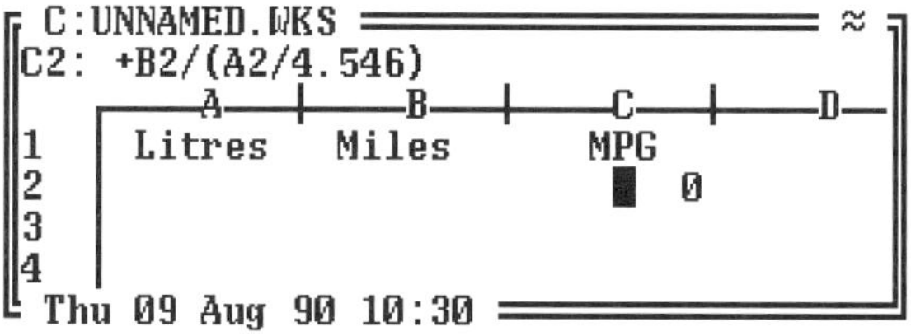

Now you can type your mileage into cell B2 and the number of litres you put in the tank into cell A2. For example, type:

in cell A2: `39` [Return]

in cell B2: `287` [Return]

Instantly, cell C2 shows the result, 33.4539 miles per gallon.

Now save your sheet using the **Files: Save as** command; perhaps using the name **mpg.wks**.

A TEMPERATURE CONVERTER

It seems that few people can relate to both Centigrade **and** Fahrenheit when measuring temperature. This small sheet allows you to type in a number in one scale and read off the equivalent in the other.

Clear the Worksheet using the **Files: New** command and enter the following information in the cells shown:

Go to Cell	Type
B1	^C
C1	^F
A2	Cent to Fahr
B2	0
C2	+(A2*9/5)+32
A3	Fahr to Cent
B3	32

C3 +(B3-32)*(5/9)

Now use the **Range: Width** command to set the width of column A to 13 characters and the width of column B and C to 7 characters.

The screen should now show:

```
C:UNNAMED.WKS                              ≈
A1: [W13]
           A          B      C        D
1                     C      F
2   Cent to Fahr>     0     32
3   Fahr to Cent>    32      0
4
 Thu 09 Aug 90 10:30
```

You can now use the converter by typing a temperature in Centigrade into cell B2 or a temperature in Fahrenheit into cell B3. The converted temperature is then immediately shown in the next cell.

Now save your sheet using the **Files: Save as** command; perhaps using the name **tempture.wks**.

A SHARE PRICE ANALYSER

This example sheet can be used to keep track of the prices of your shares. You set up the sheet by entering the names of any shares you hold, an then enter the price of each share every day. The sheet acts both as a record of the recent prices and a gauge as to how well the shares are doing.

For each share the sheet displays the lowest price of those entered, the highest price and the average price. Of course, with a sheet like this, the results generated are only as accurate and consistent as the information you type in, so do remember to type in the prices each day to make the results valid.

First, let's look at how the sheet is laid out. The first column contains the names of the shares, the next three column contain the results of the calculations on the prices and the rest of the sheet contains the daily prices:

SHARE ANALYSER

SHARE	HIGH	LOW	AVG	F	S	T	W	T	F	S
TTP Publ.	51	48	48.57	48	48	49	49	49	49	48
Petrie Prods.	178	176	177.57	178	178	178	178	178	177	176
Dart Mnfg.	310	296	301.71	300	305	310	302	302	297	296
Bell & Book	83	78	80.57	83	82	81	80	80	79	79
Ace TV.	52	49	50.42	49	50	52	51	51	50	50

The day headers run from Tuesday to Saturday because those are the days when the prices are published - for the previous day's trading.

The Sheet

Into cell A1, enter the sheet name. Running down column A, enter the names of your shares. Enter the column headers across as far as the first five day headers. Now copy the five day headers across into the rest of the sheet horizontally.

Enter the formulae:

Cell	**Type**
B5	@max(E5..DW5)
C5	@min(E5..DW5)
D5	@avg(E5..DW5)

Now copy those three cells down as far as the last of your shares names, plus a few rows, you might buy a few more shares.

All that's left to do is start entering the prices of your shares. If you miss a day, just leave that column blank. Your results will be less accurate than if every day's prices had been entered, but the rest of the prices will still be in step with the day headers.

Remember to save your sheet, perhaps using the name **shares.wks**.

A FINANCIAL FORECAST

When a business needs to look into its crystal ball and determine whether an investment is going to be a good idea, it builds a financial forecast. The Portfolio's Worksheet is perfectly equipped to help in this process. Using the Worksheet you can enter a set of figures for cash in and cash out for the duration of a new investment to see how well the investment develops.

How It Works

A financial forecast is based on just three things; money in, money out and the current balance of the bank account. These three factors are recorded in your worksheet for each month of the new investment. However, if your investment is better handled on a weekly (or even daily) basis, then the same rules apply.

For each period, be it a month, week or day, the following figures are recorded:

CASH FLOW

- Money In (positive)
- Money Out (negative)

BANK ACCOUNT

- Previous Balance (Starts at 0)
- Money In + Money Out

- Previous Balance + Money In + Money Out

The last figure is the balance of the account at the end of the current period. This total is then carried forward to the Previous Balance position for the next period.

So now let us put a six month chart together. There will be six columns of figures which follow the format shown above; a starting balance of £0.00 in the bank account and a single payment in and out for each month:

The **Money In** figures show a little cash starting to flow in after the first month, increasing as time passes. The **Money Out** figures show an initial high investment, followed by a level of expenditure which does not change.

The bottom block of figures for each period shows the bank balance at the start of the period, the sum of income and expenditure during the period and the bank balance at the

	Jan	Feb	Mar	Apr	May	Jun
Money In	0.00	3.00	7.00	12.00	17.00	25.00
Money Out	-25.00	-5.00	-5.00	-5.00	-5.00	-5.00
Previous Balance	0.00	-25.00	-27.00	-25.00	-18.00	-6.00
Money In + Money Out	-25.00	-2.00	2.00	7.00	12.00	20.00
Carried Forward	-25.00	-27.00	-25.00	-18.00	-6.00	14.00
		Greatest borrowing				Break even

end of the period. This last figure conveniently shows us the extent of any borrowing necessary during the investment. At the start of the investment when expenditure is high and little revenue is generated, the last figure in each period shows how much we must borrow from the bank. The largest negative figure shows the maximum loan we must arrange with the bank manager.

As the investment progresses and revenue starts to come in, the figures in the last row become positive; we have broken even on the investment and are now back in the black.

Now let us look at a slightly more detailed example. The Wamdidget Company has an idea for a new Didget design. The new design will have to be carefully prepared by an expensive design consultant. And then there are the new tools required to manufacture the Didget, the cost of employing a machine operator and the cost of materials.

Of course, for the first few months there will be no new income to show for all this investment. The company has a little spare capital at the moment, but is there enough to last until the revenue from Didget sales starts to come in?

This example follows the same format as the example above, but a little more detail has been added. The Money In figures are broken down into Home and Export sales and the Money Out figures have been broken down into costs for a design consultant, tooling, running costs, operator wages and materials. The Money In + Money Out figures (Net Receipts/Payments) are now taken from the total receipts plus the total payments for the month.

RECEIPTS	J	F	M	A	M	J	J
Home sales	0	1000	2000	3000	4000	4000	4000
Export sales				100	200	300	300
TOTAL	0	1000	2000	3100	4200	4300	4300
PAYMENTS							
Design Consultant	-2500						
Tooling	-1500	-500	-200				
Machine running costs		-40	-40	-40	-40	-40	-40
Operator wages	-30	-30	-30	-30	-30	-30	-30
Materials		-100	-200	-300	-400	-400	-400
TOTAL	-4030	-670	-470	-370	-470	-470	-470
Balance brought down	0	-4030	-3700	-2170	560	4290	8120
Net Receipts/Payments	-4030	330	1530	2730	3730	3830	3830
Balance carried forward	-4030	-3700	-2170	560	4290	8120	11950

The Receipts figures show that Home sales are stronger than export sales, but that both increase as time passes, up to a stable figure.

The payment to a design consultant is a one-off and the tooling costs - an initial cost plus allowances for modifications to the tools - decline to zero after three months. Other payments are on-going expenses throughout the life of the investment.

This forecast shows us that the greatest borrowing facility needed is £4030 and occurs in the first month. After three months the project breaks even and after six months shows a healthy profit.

Of course, the figures can be used to represent Pounds, Dollars, Yen, thousands, millions or any other value. Remember though that whatever units are used in one figure must also be used in the others, otherwise your results may be somewhat inaccurate!

13

PRINTING WITH POSTSCRIPT

Many offices now use laser printers instead of the old daisy-wheel or dot-matrix printers. Laser printers are quieter than impact printers and often a great deal faster. The print quality is very high and a great number of print styles are available. Some of the most impressive of these printers use the page description language PostScript.

The Portfolio's built-in software is not equipped to drive these laser printers to the limit but, with a little coaxing, the Portfolio can still use them to very good effect. This chapter includes details of a disk containing a suite of PostScript programs which, when loaded into the Portfolio, will let you print high quality documents and business graphics - even Filofax pages containing your Address Book - on any PostScript printer (or typesetting machine!).

PRINTING FROM THE PORTFOLIO

When you print from the Portfolio, whatever the destination set in the Setup facility, the output is basically the same; plain text arranged on the page using spaces and carriage returns.

Unfortunately, if you send simple text in this format to a PostScript printer, PostScript will just report an error and you will get no printout. However, you can send from the Portfolio a PostScript header, an original Portfolio file (without using any **Print** command) and then a PostScript footer. The results of such a process are shown below.

The process is as follows:

- Type in the PostScript header and footer files listed overleaf
- Type in the batch file **post.bat** overleaf
- Set a suitable line length in the Editor, set Word wrap On and type your document
- Connect your printer
- Type **post (filename) [Return]** to print.

THE POSTSCRIPT CODE

First, in DOS, when the current directory is root level, type:

```
md ps [Return]
```

This creates a new directory just to hold the two PostScript files. Now use the Editor to type in the two files. Set the **Right Margin** to 85 characters, set **Word Wrap** on - but remember to press [Return] at the end of each line. Save the files under the names given, in the directory **\ps**. See chapter 8 for full details of using the Editor.

In the body of the program, any text following a % character can be omitted, but leave in the lines at the start of the header and the end of the footer files which start %%. Text following a % character is a remark only and is not executed by PostScript.

If you are used to using other programming languages, you will be aware that every character in the program is vital. If you omit one bracket or slash or number, the program will not work. Type the program very carefully, and check it before trying it out for the first time.

FILE 1: HEADER.TXT

```
%!PS-Adobe-1.0
%%Title: POSTSCRIPT PSEUDO-DRIVER PART1
%%Creator: BARRY THOMAS
%%Pages: (atend)
%%BoundingBox: 0 0 595 841
%%EndComments
% LEFT ALIGNED TEXT
% (c) COPYRIGHT BARRY THOMAS 1988, 1989
(
```

Note that the last line ends with the opening bracket; do not press [Return] at the end of this line.

FILE 2: FOOTER.TXT

```
)
760 % position of start of text
    % 841 is the top of the page,
    % and at 72 points per inch, 760
    % is a little over an inch down.
```

```
50                          % left margin (pts)
12                          % font size (pts)

/leftalign
{
  /points exch def      % get point size
  /margin exch def      % get left margin
  /ypos exch def        % get initial y pos
  /ycur ypos def        % current y pos
  /leading              % set leading 15%
    points 1.15 mul     %   > point size
  def
  /lf 1 string def      % declare cr string
  lf 0 10 put           % set crlf string
  /Times-Roman findfont       % any font
  points scalefont setfont   % set pt size
  /newline              % line break proc
  {                     % proc start
    /ycur               % drop y pos
      ycur leading sub
    def
    margin ycur         % do a cr
    moveto
    ycur 50 lt          % ypos < 50 pts of
                        % page end? For a
                        % larger bot. margin
                        % use bigger number
    {
    /ycur ypos def      % if so, reset curr
                        % position
    showpage            % print current pg,
    margin ycur moveto % move to page head
    } if
  } def                 % end of proc
```

```
    margin ypos moveto    % move to start pt

    {                     % for all text
      lf search           % search for a lf
      {                   % if found...
        show newline pop
      }
      {exit} ifelse       % no lf found
    }
    loop
    show                  % show end of text
  } def
  leftalign
  showpage

  %%Trailer
  %%Pages: 1
  %%EOF
  ^D
```

Note that the last character in this file is a [Ctrl] [D] character. This resets PostScript to its default state at the end of your printout. To enter the ^D character, type a caret (^) followed by a D, the single character ^D appears on the screen. **Do not type in anything else after this character**.

THE BATCH FILE: POST.BAT

Now type in one of these files. If you have the optional Serial communications adapter, type in the first file. If you have the optional Parallel communications adapter, type the second file. In either case, save the file in the root level directory under the name **post.bat**.

For The Serial Adapter

```
copy \ps\header.txt com1:
copy %1 com1:
copy \ps\footer.txt com1:
```

For The Parallel Adapter

```
copy \ps\header.txt lpt1:
copy %1 lpt1:
copy \ps\footer.txt lpt1:
```

USING POST.BAT

You should now have typed:

- The first PostScript file, saved in **\ps** and called **header.txt**
- The second PostScript file, saved in **\ps** and called **footer.txt**
- One of the two batch files, saved in the root level directory and called **post.bat**.

You can now use the batch file **post.bat** as follows:

- Prepare your document in the editor
- Save the file and return to DOS
- Connect the Portfolio to your printer
- Type **post (fname) [Return]** giving the name of the file to be printed.

For example, to print out the file **home.adr** from the root level directory, type:

```
post home.adr [Return]
```

If you have difficulties printing using the Serial communications adapter, especially on larger files, try setting the **Baud** rate in the Setup option and on your printer to 1200 baud. This slows down the transfer of the programs and text to to the printer, but lessens the chance of a communications error.

MORE POSTSCRIPT

The PostScript programs in this chapter, together with the batch files and a suite of other PostScript programs are available from TTP on a 5.25" or 3.5" IBM PC format floppy disk.

The disk includes programs to print bar charts, line graphs and pie charts from Worksheet data; programs to print Diary and Address Book files in Filofax style format and programs to print text in a variety of styles - circular, shaded, italic, and so on.

To receive a copy of the disk, send a cheque to the value of £14.00 to include the disk, packing and VAT, to PS DISK, TTP Ltd, Copestake Cottage, Pinfold Lane, Bradley, ASHBOURNE, Derbyshire, DE6 1PN, UK. Please state disk format required.

14

PORTFOLIO COMMUNICATIONS

The Portfolio has a set of built-in communications programs. These allow you to transfer files between the Portfolio and a desk-top pc. To use these programs you must have one of the two communications adapters for the Portfolio. These plug into the right hand side of the computer and attach via a cable to the desk-top pc.

This section gives a brief introduction to computer communications. You don't need to know very much about computer communications at all because the Portfolio's communications software is very easy to use. However, should you want to connect the Portfolio to something other than a pc or a printer, for example a modem, a knowledge of the way computer communications works will come in very handy.

There are two sides to the subject of computer communications: the hardware and the software. The hardware is the physical connection between the computers; ie, plugs, sockets and leads. The software side concerns the speed at which the data is sent and the way in which the data is parcelled up ready for transmission.

THE HARDWARE

One way of transferring information between two dissimilar computers is by connecting them with a cable. This cable is usually plugged into an RS-232 port at each end. A standard RS-232 port consists of a number of connections used to send and receive data, and a few control lines. The port and the connectors on the ends of the cable may be either male or female. And just to make things less than simple, the connector may have 9 or 25 pins. That's all. Or at least that's all you need to know about the hardware.

When you buy one of the Portfolio's communications units, it plugs into the right hand side of the Portfolio. There are two units available, a parallel connector and a serial connector. The serial connector has a 9 pin AT style male RS232 connection. Into this you can plug a **crossed RS232 serial cable**. These are available from most computer dealers. Connect the other end of the cable to the RS-232 port on the other computer.

THE SOFTWARE

When information is transferred via an RS-232 cable, it is sent one character at a time. In fact, each character is broken down into a series of on/off pulses, which is the only way the computer can deal with data. These pulses, On (1) or Off (0), are called *Bits*, from **BI**nary digi**TS**. Eight bits are called one *Byte*. A single byte made up of eight bits stores one character; a letter, number or punctuation mark - or a space, tab or other white space character.

The software which controls the transfer of information is concerned with three main things; the speed at which the data is transferred, the format used and the method of handshaking. These three areas are explained below. The various settings which must be made for successful communication are all found within the RS-232 option in the Portfolio's Setup menu. See chapter 9 for full details of Setup.

DATA SPEED

The first and most important factor is the speed at which the data is transferred. This is usually measured in bits per second, or *Baud* (after Baudot, a telegraphy pioneer). The most commonly used speeds are 300 and 1200 for communication via a telephone line and 9600 for communication with printers and other peripherals.

DATA FORMAT

The data to be transferred must be arranged in a known format before sending, so that the receiving computer or printer can make sense of the incoming data. To do this, three different parts of the data format must be decided. The format settings must be the same on both the sending and receiving machines:

Parameter	**Valid settings**
Parity	None, Even, Odd
Data Bits	7, 8
Stop Bits	1, 2

Parity

The settings are used to select no parity (None), even parity (Even) or odd parity (Odd). A **parity bit** is an extra bit added to the data as a primitive form of error checking.

Data bits

You may use either 7 or 8 *data bits*. When communicating with comms software on a pc or sending data to a printer, it is recommended that you use 8 data bits. However, when communicating with a remote computer via a modem you may have to use 7 data bits.

Stop bits

You may use either 1 or 2 *stop bits*. The most commonly used setting is 1 stop bit.

HANDSHAKING

Commercial communications software often offers a range of *handshaking* methods. Handshaking is the process whereby the two connected computers indicate that they are ready to communicate. A full explanation of this aspect of comms is outside the scope of this book. Full details will be found in the manual which accompanies your comms software.

GOING FURTHER

This brief treatise on computer communications can only describe the generalities of comms. As was stated earlier, using the Portfolio communications adaptors requires no specialist knowledge and both adapters are supplied with full instructions for use. However, a number of excellent books on computer communications are widely availible in good book shops.

15

APPLICATION FILE FORMATS

Of the four Portfolio applications which save information in files, three use the same, plain text, format:

- The Address Book
- The Diary
- The Editor

The Worksheet saves its files in Lotus 1-2-3 format. You can load files with the extension **.wks** and **.wk1** into the Worksheet, but the Worksheet uses the default extension **.wks** when saving and loading Worksheet files.

THE ADDRESS BOOK

Address book files are saved as plain text, ASCII files, with the file extension **.adr**. Address Book files may be loaded into the Editor, examined, edited and saved.

A single Address Book entry is saved as a number of individual lines, each ending with a carriage return/line feed pair. Entries are separated by a blank line, i.e. two carriage return/line feed pairs.

The start of an Address Book file might show:

```
Andy & Susan (09696) 321
Sheep Shack House
Hilly Lane
North Yorkshire

Barbara Anne 987 6543
1873 Santa Monica Drive
Monterey
CA 98765
```

You can type names, numbers and addresses into a text file, using the Editor. The records need not be entered in alphabetical order, because the Address Book automatically sorts the file on loading. The sorted file can then be saved to a drive, when it will be saved in the correct order. Then the next time the file is loaded, the sorting process is not needed, so the file loads more quickly.

THE DIARY

Diary files are saved as plain text, ASCII files. Each date header and each entry is saved on a new line, each of which ends with a carriage return/line feed pair.

The first character on each line is always a space. The next character is either a space to denote that the entry is not a repeating entry, or one of the following:

Character	Denotes
n	non-weekend repeating (monday to friday)
d	daily repeating (all seven says)

w	weekly repeating
m	monthly repeating
y	yearly repeating

The next character is either a space which denotes that no alarm is set for that entry, or the @ character to denote an alarm entry.

If the next character is a space, the line is taken as a timed appointment entry. Otherwise the line is taken as a daily header.

The start of a Diary file might show (as seen in the Editor or by the DOS **type** command):

```
  09/08/90
d@ 10:30 Mid Morning Crisis
   10:45 Take pulse
n  11:00 Elevenses
y  12:30 Birthday Lunch with John
   15:00 Tea Time
m@ 16:00 Call accountant
  10/08/90
   17:00 T.G.I.F.
```

Note that only alarms set within the Diary file **diary.dry** stored in the directory called **\system** will sound. See chapter 7 for further details of using the Diary.

THE EDITOR

Editor files are saved a plain text, ASCII files, with a carriage return/line feed pair at the end of each word wrapped line, at the point of the end of line as displayed in the Editor. This means that it doesn't matter where your end-of-line markers are in the saved document, the document is always formatted to the current margin setting in the Editor.

Lines ended by pressing [Return] are saved as a carriage return/line feed pair without a preceding space.

THE WORKSHEET

The Worksheet loads files saved in Lotus 1-2-3 release 1A and release 2.

The functions available in Lotus 1-2-3 which are not supported by the Portfolio Worksheet are listed below.

Database statistical:

@DAVG	@DDB	@DCOUNT	@DMAX
@DMIN	@DSTD	@DSUM	@DVAR

String handling:

@CHAR	@CLEAN	@CODE	@EXACT
@FIND	@ISNUMBER	@ISSTRING	@LEFT
@LENGTH	@LOWER	@MID	@N
@PROPER	@REPEAT	@REPLACE	@RIGHT
@S	@STRING	@TRIM	@UPPER
@VALUE			

Others:

@CELLPOINTER	@CELL	@COLS	@CTERM
@HOUR	@MINUTE	@ROWS	@RATE
@SECOND	@SLN	@SYD	@TERM
@TIME			

If you load a Lotus 1-2-3 file which uses any of these functions, the Worksheet will display the message **Some data cannot be loaded**. Formulae containing unsupported functions are replaced with the function @ERR. Graphics information included with a Lotus 1-2-3 is ignored by the Worksheet.

16

THE PORTFOLIO ERROR MESSAGES

When you are using the built-in applications, the Portfolio will occasionally display a message on the screen, shown in the usual double-lined window. The message might be to alert you to some error or other important condition. Also, when you type a command in DOS, the Portfolio may respond with a message if there is some problem with the command you typed. These are the Portfolio's error messages.

If an error message is displayed in a window, press [Esc] to cancel the message and return to what you were doing when the error occurred. If you are in DOS and an error message is displayed, the message may tell you what to do; otherwise see the error in the list below.

GETTING OUT OF TROUBLE

If the Portfolio starts an operation which you decide you would rather not have happen, there are a number of options open to you; if you are in DOS, you can press [Ctrl] [C] or [Fn] [B] to break into an activity. If the problem is more serious, hold down [Ctrl], [Alt] and [Del/Ins] together to reset the computer. If this does not work, press the reset button on the bottom of the Portfolio's casing. If all else fails, remove the batteries, press the reset button and reinsert the batteries.

THE ERROR MESSAGES

Access denied

You have attempted to delete or edit a file which has been designated 'Read Only'. This cannot happen if you are just using the built-in applications. However, it might happen if you transfer a Read Only file from a desk-top pc to the Portfolio.

Bad command or program not found

In DOS you typed something which was neither a legal DOS command or the name of a program on any of the available drives, which the Portfolio could execute.

Check the spelling of the command. If the command was the name of a batch file, check that the DOS **path** command allows the batch file to be found.

Bad filename

In the applications or in DOS you have specified a file name which is illegal. File names may be up to 8 letters and numbers long, with an optional file extension of up to three letters or numbers. See chapter 4 for full details of legal file names.

Bad number

One of two things has happened; you typed something other than a number when a number was expected, or you typed a number outside the range allowed by the Portfolio. Numbers in the Calculator and Worksheet must be in the range plus or minus 9.9999 to the power 99.

Bad or corrupted CONFIG.SYS

Your **config.sys** file either contains an illegal command or the file has been corrupted. Check the contents of the file. Chapter 4 contains details of valid commands for this file.

Bad or missing <x>

Where <x> is a device driver, such as **ansi.sys**. Device drivers may be specified in the **config.sys** file, using the **device=** command. If a specified driver is not found in the current path, this message is displayed.

BASIC not available

A program has attempted to run the program called BASIC which was built into the original IBM PC. This is not available on the Portfolio. This error will never occur if you are just using the Portfolio's built in applications.

Cannot create file

In DOS you attempted to create a file whose name contained illegal characters or was missing. See chapter 4 for full details of legal file names.

Cannot move - target day is occupied

In the Diary, you attempted to use the **Move** command to move a date header to a date which already has a date header.

Checksum error

An error was found in the checksum - a form of error checking device - while using the file transfer facility within Setup. Make sure the communications adapter is correctly fitted; check the cable is plugged in firmly and try again.

Communications error

This message is displayed if you select the **Initialize!** option in the RS-232 section of Setup. It may also appear if an error occurs during a file transfer. Check the connections as in the above error.

Configuration too large for memory

If you specify a system configuration, using commands in the **config.sys** file, which requires more memory than the Portfolio can afford, then this message is displayed. Reduce the number of commands in the **config.sys** file and try again.

Corrupt file

If you try to load a file created in Lotus 1-2-3 which has somehow been corrupted, this message will appear. Try saving the file again in Lotus, transfer the new copy to the Portfolio and try to load it again.

Data error reading/writing drive <x>

Abort, Retry, Ignore?

If a memory card has been corrupted, perhaps it was left near a motor or a magnet (even the magnet in a hi-fi speaker!), the data stored on the card cannot be read and this error will occur. If a memory card has had the battery removed, it reverts to the state it was in when it was first purchased. Again, this error will be displayed.

Press [A] to Abort the attempt to read the card and use the DOS **format** command to reformat the memory card ready for use.

Date repeat skipped as target day occupied

When you load a Diary file, the repeating entries are automatically rearranged as necessary. The Diary attempted to make a date header repeat, but the target date already has a date header. The date header is moved forwards until a free date is found.

Device Read Error

Either you removed a memory card while the Portfolio was trying to read information from it, or you specified a non-existent directory as part of a path name. See chapter 4 for full details of path names.

You should never remove a memory card while the Portfolio is reading information from it. Check that the card is fully inserted or check that the path name is correct.

Device write failure

The Portfolio attempted to write information to a memory card or the internal drive and failed. The drive (or memory card) may be full; the directory given as part of a path name may not exist or the memory card may not be correctly inserted.

Directory exists or cannot be created

Using the DOS **md** command, you attempted to create a directory which either already exists or a file by that name already exists.

Directory not found or not empty

To remove a directory from a drive, use the DOS **rd** command. However, first make sure that the directory is empty. This error occurs if there are files in the directory to be removed or the directory is not found.

Disk full

Either the internal drive or a memory card is full. This error occurs if you try to copy files to a memory device which is full.

Disk is write protected

Memory cards have a small switch on one end. This is the Write Protect switch. If the switch is set to Off, you cannot write information to the card or delete existing information. Set the switch to Off and try again.

Divide by zero

If you are running an external program and an internal error occurs, this error may occur. Quit from the program and run it again. If the Portfolio 'hangs', i.e. does not respond to normal commands on the keyboard, hold down [Ctrl], [Alt] and [Del/Ins] together to reset the computer.

Drive in search path not found

You have specified a drive as part of the DOS **path** command which is not available.

Enter new drive

For some reason the current drive cannot be used, enter a new drive letter and press [Return].

Environment full

The DOS commands **prompt**, **path** and **set** have been used to the extent that the area of memory (the environment) assigned for their use has been filled. Remove some of the settings before attempting to re-use these commands to make new settings.

ERROR: Card access

When the Portfolio was reading or writing information on a memory card, the card was removed from the drive. You should never remove a memory card while the Portfolio is reading or writing information on the card.

ERROR: Low battery

The Portfolio's batteries are too low to power the computer. Remove the batteries and replace them with fresh ones. Be wise - always carry a spare set of batteries! See chapter 1 for further information.

Exec error

An executable file (with the extension **.exe**) has been corrupted or has insufficient memory to run. This error will never occur if you are only using the Portfolio's built-in applications.

Failed to run program

A program used as an add-in to the Editor could not run; either because the file has been corrupted or because there was insufficient memory for it to run.

File not found

Either a command issued in DOS specified a non-existent file, (check the spelling of the file name and/or check the directory; or you specified a non-existent file to be loaded into an application.

FOR cannot be nested

The DOS **for** command cannot be used as part of another **for** command.

Format error

The DOS **format** command failed to correctly format a memory card. Remove the card, carefully replace it in the drive and try again.

Formula too long

In the Worksheet, you typed a formula which is too long for the cell. Break the formula down into smaller sections and rearrange the sheet accordingly. Your sheet will be easier to use and understand if the formulae are of a reasonable length.

General error reading/writing drive <x>

Abort, Retry, Ignore?

If a memory card has been partially corrupted, perhaps it was left near a motor or a magnet (even the magnet in a hi-fi speaker!), the data stored on the card cannot be read and this error will occur. If a memory card has had the battery removed, it reverts to the state it was in when it was first purchased. Again, this error will be displayed.

Halt batch job (Y/N)?

If you halt a batch file by holding down [Ctrl] and pressing [C], or holding down [Fn] and pressing [B], DOS checks that you want to end execution of the batch file. Press [Y] and press [Return] to halt the batch file; press [N] and press [Return] to continue execution of the batch file.

Illegal cell reference

In the Worksheet you typed either a bad cell reference (for example, A1B) or a cell reference which oversteps the limits of the grid. The grid extends to cell DW255.

Illegal character

In the Calculator, this error is displayed if any character other than a legal arithmetic operator or number is typed. See chapter 6 for full details on using the calculator.

Illegal date

Either in the Diary or in DOS an illegal date was specified. Dates must be specified according to the country code set in your **config.sys** file. See chapter 4 for full details of this file.

Illegal time

Either in the Diary or in DOS an illegal time was specified. Times must be specified in the form hh:mm:ss:xx, where the hours follow the 24 hour format and where xx is the number of hundredths of a second. The end parts of the time may be omitted.

Insert disk with batch file

A batch file was run from a memory card, and then the memory card removed. Reinsert the memory card to allow the batch file to continue. Alternatively, a batch file may have deleted itself during execution, perhaps by a **del a:*.*** command or similar. Press [Ctrl] [C] to terminate the batch file.

Internal disk error

An error occurred when the Portfolio was formatting the internal drive. Remove the batteries, press the small reset button on the base of the basing and replace the batteries.

Invalid characters in label

The DOS **label** command allows you to assign a volume label to a drive. The label must be no more than 11 characters long and cannot contain any spaces. Check the label and re-enter the command.

Invalid country code

Your **config.sys** file contains a country code which is invalid. See chapter 4 for the list of valid country codes.

Invalid directory

When using the DOS commands **dir** or **cd** an invalid directory name was specified. Check the directory name and try again.

Invalid drive

One of a number of DOS commands might report this error if an invalid drive specifier is given. Check your **config.sys** file and any command just typed.

Invalid parameter

One of a number of DOS commands has been given an invalid parameter. Look up the description of the DOS command in chapter 4. Also, the Worksheet may report this error when a function is given the wrong type of parameter. See chapter 11 for full details of the Worksheet functions.

Label not found

Batch files may use the DOS **goto** command which redirects program execution. The **goto** command uses a label as the destination. If the label does not exist in the current batch file, this error is reported. Check the spelling of the label.

Max size allowed is <n>k

When you use the DOS **fdisk** command, if you exceed the maximum size allowed for the internal RAM drive, this error message is displayed, showing the maximum size. Try again using a smaller size.

Memory full

An external program was run which requires more memory than is currently available on the Portfolio. Alternatively a large file was loaded into one of the built-in applications and the Portfolio ran out of memory.

If you use any memory resident programs, remove them to make more memory available and/or try to split your data file into several smaller ones.

If this message appears while you are using one of the built-in applications, you can free some memory by deleting the files **undelete.dat** and **clipbord.dat** from the directory **\system**. See chapter 2 for more details of these files.

Minimum drive size <n>k

Using the **fdisk** command you attempted to create a RAM drive of less than the minimum size. Try again using a larger size.

Mismatched brackets

In the Worksheet or the Calculator, an expression was entered with an uneven number of brackets (there should be one close bracket for every open bracket). Check the expression for a missing or extraneous bracket.

Missing operator +-*/^!

In the Calculator, one of the operators indicated is required at the position shown, for the calculation to make sense.

Must specify on or off

The DOS commands **break** and **verify** must only be used with the parameters **on** or **off**. Check the command and try again.

Must specify source and target files

When using the **copy** command in DOS, the source and destination file names must both be specified and they must not be the same.

No path

If the DOS **path** command is issued with no parameters, DOS reports the current path. If the message **No path** is displayed, there is no path currently in use. Set a path with the DOS commands **path** or **set**.

Not ready error reading/writing drive

Abort, Retry, Ignore?

In DOS if you attempt to read or write to a memory card when there is no card in the drive, or if the Portfolio's power became low during a read/write operation, this message will be displayed.

Press [A] to Abort the attempt to read the card and try again.

Out of range

A number of errors can cause this message to be displayed. For example, if a number is entered which falls outside an expected range, perhaps you entered a top margin of 25 lines when the maximum is 20 in **Setup: Printer**.

Ram check failure

The Portfolio has detected an error in its memory during start-up. Remove the batteries and press the reset button on the bottom of the casing; reinsert the batteries and start again.

Root directory full

The root level directory on a drive is full. Delete some of the files on the drive to create more room, or make a sub-directory to contain further files.

Second drive not installed

The **format** command has been used to attempt to format a memory card in the second drive, when the second drive is not attached.

Some alarms are set in the past and so will not go off

When you exit from the Diary, saving the file as **\system\diary.dry**, if any of the entries with dates or times before the current Portfolio time have associated alarms, this warning is displayed.

Stack full

A calculation attempted in the Calculator was too complex for the Portfolio to evaluate. Break the calculation down into smaller parts and try again.

String not found

The **Search** command was used in one of the applications but the search was unsuccessful and the text was not found. To search forwards, end the search string with [↓]; to search backwards, use [↑].

Syntax error

You typed a DOS command or a calculation in the Calculator or Worksheet which was badly formed. Check the calculation or the command and try again.

Target file exists

When using the **ren** (rename) command, you attempted to rename a file with a name which is already in use. Try again with a different destination file name.

Target is over the edge

The **copy** command in the worksheet was used to copy a number of cells onto a range which would overlap one or more edges of the grid. You must specify a smaller block of cells which fits inside the room you have available, or use a different area of the grid.

Too may cols or rows

If you attempt to insert enough rows or columns into the Worksheet, such that information would be pushed off one or more edges of the grid, this message is displayed and the insertion fails.

Unrecognised command in CONFIG.SYS

Your **config.sys** file contains a command which DOS does not support. See chapter 4 for the range of commands allowed in this file.

WARNING!
Alarms won't ring - must
be in C:\SYSTEM\DIARY.DRY

If you set any Diary alarms in a file other than the one shown in the message, this warning is displayed when you leave the Diary. See chapter 7 for full details of how Diary alarms work.

WARNING!
Monthly repeat has been moved
due to earlier end of month

Monthly repeats in the Diary which fall close to the end of a month may be moved to an earlier day of the month if the target day does not exist (e.g. 29, 30, 31 February and so on.)

WARNING!

Some data cannot be loaded

The Worksheet does not support all of the Lotus 1-2-3 release 2 functions. If you load a sheet containing any of these functions, this message is displayed. See chapters 11 and 15 for full details of the Worksheet functions.

Write protect error writing drive

Abort, Retry, Ignore?

Memory cards have a small switch on one end. This is the Write Protect switch. If the switch is set to Off, you cannot write information to the card or delete existing information. Set the switch to Off and try again.

Wrong number of params

If a DOS command or a Worksheet function is given the wrong number of parameters, this message will be displayed. See chapter 4 for details of the DOS command syntax and chapter 11 for the Worksheet functions' syntax.

** SYSTEM ERROR ** Sorry!

Note what you last did;

ESC will attempt recovery.

Quit & save if possible

In all computer products there comes the time when an error occurs which no-one could have predicted. This error message is used by the Portfolio to indicate that something quite unexpected occurred. Press [Esc] to clear the message. If it can, the Portfolio will return you to the previous activity. If you were using an application, save the file and return to DOS.

Occasionally this may not be possible. The next step is to hold down the [Ctrl], [Alt] and [Del/Ins] keys together. This performs a reset on the Portfolio. If that does not produce results, press the rest button on the bottom of the casing. If all else fails, remove any memory card in the drive, disconnect any other peripherals and remove the batteries. Reinsert the batteries and try again.

APPENDIX A

THE ASCII CHARACTERS

The table overleaf shows all of the Portfolio's printable characters. To find the decimal ASCII (*American Standard Code for Information Interchange*) code for any character, look at the number at the top of the column in which the character lies; multiply this number by sixteen; add the number at the left of the row in which the character lies. This gives you a number between 1 and 255. This number can be used to insert any of these characters into one of your files, as described in chapter 8.

At the top of the columns at the right of the table and at the left of the rows at the bottom of the table, the numbers change to letters. The numbers 10, 11, 12, 13, 14 and 15 are represented by A, B, C, D, E and F respectively. This is called *Hexadecimal notation* and is widely used in the world of computers.

	0	1	2	3	4	5	6	7	8	9	A	B	C	D	E	F
0			SP	0	@	P	`	p	Ç	É	á	░	└	╨	α	≡
1			!	1	A	Q	a	q	ü	æ	í	▒	┴	╤	β	±
2			"	2	B	R	b	r	é	Æ	ó	▓	┬	╥	Γ	≥
3			#	3	C	S	c	s	â	ô	ú	│	├	╙	π	≤
4			$	4	D	T	d	t	ä	ö	ñ	┤	─	╘	Σ	⌠
5			%	5	E	U	e	u	à	ò	Ñ	╡	┼	╒	σ	⌡
6			&	6	F	V	f	v	å	û	ª	╢	╞	╓	µ	÷
7			'	7	G	W	g	w	ç	ù	º	╖	╟	╫	τ	≈
8			(	8	H	X	h	x	ê	ÿ	¿	╕	╚	╪	Φ	°
9			)	9	I	Y	i	y	ë	Ö	⌐	╣	╔	┘	Θ	∙
A			*	:	J	Z	j	z	è	Ü	¬	║	╩	┌	Ω	·
B			+	;	K	[	k	{	ï	¢	½	╗	╦	█	δ	√
C			,	<	L	\	l	¦	î	£	¼	╝	╠	▄	∞	ⁿ
D			-	=	M	]	m	}		¥	¡	╜	═	▌	φ	²
E			.	>	N	^	n	~	Ä	₧	«	╛	╬	▐	ε	■
F			/	?	O	_	o		Å	ƒ	»	┐	╧	▀	∩	

INDEX